A Vision for the Future

A Vision for the Future

In Conversation with Financial Strategists

Edited by

Luc Keuleneer, Dirk Swagerman, and Willem Verhoog

JOHN WILEY & SONS, LTD

Chichester • New York • Weinheim • Brisbane • Singapore • Toronto

This edition published in 2001 by   John Wiley & Sons Ltd,
Baffins Lane, Chichester,
West Sussex PO19 1UD, England

National   01243 779777
International   (+44) 1243 779777
e-mail (for orders and customer service enquiries):
cs-books@wiley.co.uk
Visit our Home Page on http://www.wiley.co.uk

First published in 2000 by Royal NIVRA, Amsterdam
Copyright © 2000 Royal Nivra, Amsterdam

Other Wiley Editorial Offices

John Wiley & Sons Inc., 605 Third Avenue,
New York, NY 10158-0012, USA

WILEY-VCH Verlag GmbH, Pappelallee 3,
D-69469 Weinheim, Germany

Jacaranda Wiley Ltd, 33 Park Road, Milton,
Queensland 4064, Australia

John Wiley & Sons (Asia) Pte Ltd, 2 Clementi Loop #02-01,
Jin Xing Distripark, Singapore 129809

John Wiley & Sons (Canada) Ltd, 22 Worcester Road,
Rexdale, Ontario M9W 1L1, Canada

British Library Cataloguing in Publication Data

A catalogue record for this book is available from the British Library

ISBN 0-471-49785-1

Typeset in Plantin by Footnote Graphics, Warminster, Wilts.
Printed and bound in Great Britain by Antony Rowe Ltd, Chippenham

This book is printed on acid-free paper responsibly manufactured from sustainable forestation, for which at least two trees are planted for each one used for paper production.

Contents

Preface

The Dutch-language book 'Fifteen on Finance' appeared in 1996. This publication, by the Royal NIVRA's Continuing Professional Education Committee (VERA), was so favourably received that it sold out almost immediately and a second reprint quickly followed. Because of the rapid developments in the financial world a third edition was ruled out and it was decided to produce a totally new publication in the same field, although this time based on a wider perspective. That's the reason why in this publication the context is more international. The contributors include two Nobel Prize winners, Professors Harry Markowitz and Merton Miller. Other international experts who were asked to give their vision about the field are Professors Shlomo Benartzi (behavioural finance) and Tom Copeland (valuation).

The editors are proud to be able to include contributions from other experts in the financial field (Bilderbeek, Dorsman, Feenstra, Glasz, Hommen, Van den Goorbergh, Keuleneer, De Korte, Lintjer, Meijer, Van Steenberge, Swagerman, Thibeault, Traas). We are also very honoured to be able to include a contribution by the Dutch Minister of Finance, Mr. Zalm.

The editors would like to take this opportunity to express their gratitude for the co-operation and the contributions that they received from all those mentioned above. After reading this book, it will be apparent to all that it was both a privilege and a pleasure to become acquainted with their ideas and opinions.

On behalf of the editors,
Willem Verhoog
October 2000

A vision for the future: an introduction

This book *A Vision for the Future: in conversation with financial strategists* deals with the content and consequences of Strategic Finance. This term is understood as: 'the employment of corporate finance and financial management by means of responsible management in order to achieve optimal financial control'. From this description it already appears that the term 'Strategic Finance' must be considered in a broad context. If only corporate finance is looked at, internal financial management will be ignored. It is therefore a question of the way in which management bears the ultimate responsibility for financial policy and is able to use this policy strategically in realising organisational objectives. This responsibility is a generic responsibility and not only a responsibility that ensues from sound financial management practice. Keuleneer and Van Steenberge scrutinise the theoretical background, which is the basic principle of modern corporate finance and thinking in terms of the creation of value.

This requires a more detailed explanation. When business organisations are looked at, it is assumed that the management must serve the interests of the provider of the capital. This generic aim has been criticised by a number of those interviewed. Bilderbeek and Swagerman take a detailed look at a number of theoretical considerations. Despite the criticism that the creation of shareholder value applies only to a limited number of enterprises, companies are assiduously searching for activities which create value. It is the Number One starting point in the field of modern management. This is dealt with in detail in the interview with Feenstra concerning the functioning of the international capital market. The boards of companies cannot afford to ignore thinking about shareholder value. What is the reason for this? Probably it is a logical consequence of the manner the society in which we live is arranged. The creation of goods and services takes place through the market. The market, with its 'invisible hand' ensures, ideally, for an optimal allocation. Subsequently, this optimal allocation must result in the acquisition of the greatest possible degree of welfare. Achieving this objective demands the application of 'the art of management'. It appears, furthermore, that progress in information technology also exercises influence on the financial function. An increasing number of 'finance/IT' products are being created.

The market is not always fair and perfect in all cases. It is also a fact that not everything can be left to market forces. This is why there is government intervention. In the case in question, this applies in particular to the banking industry. If the banking industry were to be subject fully and exclusively to the discipline of the market, the risk of insolvency would increase. Society demands a solid and stable financial sector. In view of the economic and social developments, a shift is occurring in the nature of the disciplinary bodies. There is evidence of an increase of international supervision and there is a tendency noted towards a combining of forces of the individual sector supervisors for the financial sector.

The behaviour of the market cannot be predicted. If we could predict market behaviour, there would be opportunities to obtain superior returns. Since this is not the case, account must always be taken of uncertainties and therefore of risks and volatility.

There are organisations that fall insufficiently, or not at all, within the working of the market mechanism. Charity foundations are a good example. Doesn't Strategic Finance also apply to them? It does, but not to the same degree as to business. Charity foundations can allow themselves to be guided by considerations that are not strictly financial. It is a fact, however, that this type of organisation must be careful with its scarce financial resources because the revenue must after all reach the intended goals. Sound financial management practice is the means of ensuring that sufficient resources will achieve these goals.

In this book, a detailed look is taken at the manner in which organisations are working with Strategic Finance. A clear overview is presented of contemporary management philosophies, the way in which the creation of value is being sought in all kinds of fields. Opinions from the academic world are subsequently presented, together with the opinion of government. These viewpoints present a rich source for arriving at conclusions concerning the relevance of Strategic Finance. What is the most important conclusion of the interviews? It appears that by means of Strategic Finance, a relationship can be established between corporate strategy and financial management. In the past these two domains were separate; now the gap between them has been bridged. This aspect must emerge as the guiding principle from the various interviews. Theoretically speaking, the (real) option approach in particular provides in the link between management decision making and the financial consequences which accompany it.

In the interviews, a number of recurring themes can be discovered, i.e. matters relating to Strategic Finance. In the epilogue (page 179–181), these trends and developments are looked at once again.

Shareholder value and Value Based Management

The importance of shareholder value can be seen as one of the most important aspects of strategic financial management. From the information emerging from the interviews, it appears that the majority of the organisations are aiming at value creation. It is very interesting to see how Philips deals with Value Based Management (VBM). Mr. Hommen indicates clearly that the management is acting not only in the interest of the shareholder, but must also achieve the internal creation of value. Traas also underlines the importance of VBM and even goes a step further: management must provide insight into its plans for the future. In the US, this is already normal for companies under the SEC regime, but here in Europe this example is followed reluctantly. The shareholders, due to their interest in the stock-quoted company based their knowledge on external reporting. The annual reports must present a picture directed towards the future.

Nevertheless, it is possible to introduce certain nuances into all these opinions. There are also organisations without shareholders which are striving to introduce an equivalent concept. This can be seen from the interview with Van den Goorbergh from the Rabobank. The bank has no shareholders but it has control over market shares in the capacity of 'consumer value'. In addition, the following can be said about the primacy of the shareholders compared to other stakeholders. In the 'Rhineland model', much value is attached to the relationship between all those involved in the company. When viewed from the 'Balanced scorecard' approach, it appears that in addition to the reporting concerning financial progress, other aspects are also included. This can be regarded as an appreciable broadening of the view based on shareholder value thinking alone, in the opinions concerning, and consideration of organisations.

Dorsman and Thibeault examine the necessity of risk management in organisations. In that context it is important to look at the difference in the approaches selected by organisations, i.e. the purely shareholder-oriented approach or the more stakeholder-oriented one. An important aspect of risk management is applying the 'Value at Risk' approach. All banks have, by now, set up a 'Value at Risk' system. As stated above, organisations are striving to create value. To achieve this, it is necessary that the return on the invested capital is higher than the WACC.

It speaks volumes when Hommen says that a company only creates value as the result of the expectation of the providers of the capital. It appears that, certainly at Philips, striving to create value is the prime aim. In line with Hommen, Copeland admits that the 'value added' lies in the difference between what is actually achieved and the expectations of the providers of the capital. In the US, databases are available which set out the expectations of the analysts concerning the development of the 'return on invested capital'. These developments could meet with Copeland's approval, although he is of the opinion that more things need to be included in these expectations.

As far as the developments in the field of the evaluation of assets is concerned, certain things have to be said. The credo is still the use of the Discounted Cash Flow (DCF) method. While this is theoretically correct, the technique has a number of shortcomings. In the first place, replacing the Weighted Average Cost of Capital (WACC) by making use of the 'adjusted present value' would produce an improvement. It is difficult for an organisation to estimate future cash flows. Determining the residual value is difficult, too. Therefore, Copeland also sees more in the future use of the 'real options' approach for the solving of this problem. In the interview with Miller, he notes that the expectation in the coming years is that real options will be of vital importance.

Philips was one of the first companies to apply an extensive system of value creating techniques. VBM is seen as one of the most important instruments for achieving the creation of value. Traas is a supporter of upgrading the shareholder value of which VBM is a means of putting this into practice.

According to Traas: in order to realise VBM, targets must be formulated in terms of Economic Value Added (EVA). The EVA concepts must be correct and, in this context, it is also important to determine the value drivers in the company. The criticism of the EVA concept is that when it is applied correctly, the results obtained are the same as those generated by the DCF method. The DCF method gives a total figure when one looks at the value of a project. In the EVA approach this value is built up more gradually. Traas is of the opinion that this favours a sound selection of projects since a clearer picture of developments emerges. The effort of researchers to find a correlation between EVA and share price is futile according to Traas: 'Share prices do not only react to the outcome of a single financial year, but rather to expectations for a series of years in future. Being an internal performance indicator, EVA can never correspond perfectly with share prices'. This can also be linked to the well-known opinion of Markowitz concerning an 'efficient market hypothesis'. We cannot beat the market and therefore share prices cannot be predicted with any certainty. The other Nobel prize winner Miller also illustrates the importance of theoretical insight into the application of Strategic Finance. Tactical knowledge on its own is not sufficient; knowledge of the theoretical background is also needed. In various capacities, organisations are engaged in introducing this type of management technique. The expectation is therefore that these will be further developed in the future and will remain topical for quite some time to come.

Meijer considers the fact that there is more than just shareholder value. The use of shareholder value must not be an end in itself. The concept must be placed in a broader context. People are involved who are together trying to shape the organisation. This is important and must not ignored. At Nedlloyd, a lot of things are happening, there has been a tremendous turn-around, which has been achieved by pursuing a clear financial policy. Nedlloyd succeeded in introducing the concepts of VBM by keeping the capacity as tight as possible and thus not growing too fast since the cashflow would otherwise be endangered. The starting point for Nedlloyd is that the business cashflow must be positive.

Corporate Governance

The phenomenon of Corporate Governance is also something that people are concerned with. The general opinion is that attention for Corporate Governance has not yet reached its zenith. Following the initial interest in the concept, attention shifted to the institutionalisation of the interpretations of Corporate Governance in organisations. If we look at the 'forty recommendations' of the Peters Committee, not all of them have been adopted *con amore* by the management. Nevertheless, a solution must be arrived at in order to bring the discussion, which is still going on, to a positive conclusion. A number of dimensions can be distinguished in the phenomenon of Corporate Governance. In the first place, is the fact that there has to be accountability. In the second place, there is the question of the transparency of the policy. In addition, there has to be certainty and predictability of rules and policy. Ultimately, the entire discussion on Corporate Governance results in a greater ethical sense and, in the context of this publication, in a higher morality in the implementation of the financial function. It is not true that thinking about Corporate Governance is strictly limited to the business community. The public sector is also concerned with Governance. There, it is a question of 'sound management' in general and most certainly in the financial operations. Many people are of the opinion that a migration to the Anglo-Saxon model would be appropriate for a number of European countries. With this, they are referring to a situation in which more demands are made on the transparency of corporate policy and where the shareholder is more closely involved in policy.

It is also predicted that the influence of the US will become more widely felt in Europe as far as demands with respect to annual reporting are concerned. It is interesting to note that in future, most certainly stimulated by the fruits of information technology, ideas on the use of the annual report will evolve and take on a new form. Certainly in the case of annual reporting guidelines, a number of things could still be tightened up by having stricter guidelines, bringing them into line with practice in the US. A non-committal attitude is far too widespread. As far as management reporting is concerned, there is certainly room for improvement. In the US, there is the MD&A report that even provides information about future prospects. Several European countries such as the Netherlands, could benefit from a move towards this kind of development. Transparency of reporting results in greater certainty for the investor, which makes it easier to attract capital. In that sense, corporate governance could contribute to the value of the company.

Also within Nedlloyd, corporate governance plays an important role. Meijer has reservations about certain matters, however. He considers the recommendations of the Peters Committee as positive, but he would not wish to adopt all of them as they stand. There is, and continues to be, a discrepancy between the interest of the company, as represented by the Executive Board, and the interest of the shareholder. Therefore, in Meijer's opinion, it is not right for the shareholder to determine what happens in the company. A close examination needs to be made of the way in which the shareholders' meeting operates. It must certainly not be the case that a proxy solicitation comes into effect on the basis of 'one man one vote'. Decisions would then be taken on the basis of the majority of votes cast without any discussion of the content. In Meijer's opinion, this is not the direction in which we should be heading.

Supervision

Supervision is also examined. More attention will definitely need to be paid to this in the future. In the Netherlands, for example, supervision is spread over a number of bodies. This does not contribute to transparency. There will need to be changes in this field in the future. These changes will need to be linked to those taking place on the European scale.

When matters such as transparency are considered, it has to be realised that no country can behave as an island. The opinion of Mr. Zalm, the Dutch Minister of Finance, is that this can be seen from the convergence of the European economies and as a result of the linking of the European bourses. Van den Goorbergh, as an advocate of the subsidiarity principle of supervision, notes that it is desirable that supervision takes place at a national level. But this must be within a framework of international agreements. The interview with Van den Goorbergh also makes it clear that the Rabobank is currently focusing strongly on achieving an 'all finance' concept. This also means that the bank still has to cope with a number of different supervisors. The Minister of Finance makes a number of interesting remarks about the possibility of cross-border mergers.

The opinion of Glasz is that, in the final analysis, the question is how the activities are organised. This applies not only to the objective of shareholder value but also to supervision. The leading criterion is 'proper'. The problem which now arises is that this term is not sufficiently clearly specified. Because to this, the term 'proper' is interpreted differently in practice by accountants, lawyers and academics, according to their own insights. Over time, the content of the terms 'proper administration' and 'proper supervision' are changing.

The Peters Committee makes an important contribution by interpreting the content of these concepts. The work of the Peters Committee has had considerable influence on the thinking about the relationship between an organisation and its stakeholders. Because of the open character of its economy, the Netherlands closely follows international developments. The supervision of the company is carried out by the Supervisory Board. In addition, the members of the Supervisory Board have the task of advising the company. The two-tier system of supervision is common in the Netherlands. The members of the Supervisory Board perform their task in an independent manner. It is not expected that this system will be subjected to the pressure of European harmonisation in the near future. Elsewhere, in particular in the Anglo-Saxon countries, there is a 'one-tier system'. Here, there are executive and non-executive directors. Fortis provides us with an example of this system. The one-tier system will require a different position on legal liability. There is a difference between the two types of executives. The

7

executive directors have a lot more information at their disposal than the non-executive directors. The current legal framework is based on the Supervisory Board member who bears the full responsibility since he is an executive and therefore not a supervisor. This is naturally not a viable situation. Legal amendments will be necessary in the system of liability.

Another point is the knowledge gap, which can occur in the case of members of the Supervisory Board. Look at the current discussion on management options. Is the supervisor sufficiently conscious of the technical aspects of option schemes? Not in all cases, probably. For the adequate exercise of supervision, insight is needed or there must be a possibility of obtaining the necessary insight. It is increasingly evident that being a Supervisory Board member is becoming a professional career.

The volume of worldwide capital flows is increasing. Also from the point of view of supervision there is every reason to be very alert. The argument to levy tax on capital flows (Tobin argument), which would reduce these flows to some extent, does not receive much support, however.

Many of those interviewed talk about derivatives. They particularly point to the risks of inexpert use of derivatives, but nevertheless their use is generally regarded as a positive development. Derivatives are used to hedge positions but also to realise additional profit. This potential is the reason that there has been such a big increase in their use. In many cases this causes the supervisor a lot of concern. The BIS is constantly tightening the guidelines with regard to the use of derivatives by banking institutions. At the moment, it is impossible to tell whether these measures are adequate. A positive development is that there has been a decline in the number of disasters caused by the inexpert use of derivatives. This is perhaps particularly the consequence of the increase of the level of knowledge and the further perfection of business controls.

Supervision is very important in relation to the large consortia, which generate the 'all finance' concept. A phenomenon is occurring which is known as 'moral hazard'; the bigger the financial institution the greater the risk it can cope with. A bankruptcy will no longer occur since in that case there would be a domino effect, something to be avoided at all costs. In fact, these 'all finance' consortia are therefore virtually invulnerable to the dangers that accompany unjustified risk.

Derivatives

If we look at derivatives, in a perfectly efficient market additional profit will not be obtained by the use of derivatives. For, in that case, risk can only be shifted elsewhere; it cannot be eliminated. In order to shift the risk, costs must be incurred for the financial instruments. Value creation can be achieved with the use of derivatives only in those specific circumstances in which market imperfections can be countered.

It does appear, however, that Strategic Finance in the future will be increasingly led by derivative applications. The developments in the field of real options are, in this context, certainly promising and interesting. The approach whereby each management decision can be seen as an option, namely the choice between deciding or not deciding, has far-reaching implications. In this respect, the value of alternatives must be given. The more uncertain the circumstances, the greater the related value. This new form of thinking will certainly have an influence.

International institutional banks

The Netherlands is well represented in the various international institutional banks. In this context, we will look in detail at the interviews with two bank representatives.

Where the Asian crisis is concerned, Lintjer from the Asian Development Bank believes that there will be a revival of the Asian economies that have been affected. It is highly likely that the crisis will result in Asian countries attempting to have greater transparency in their financial policy and also open up their economies to a greater degree. In addition, the disasters of recent years have resulted in the tendency for a 'clean sweep' in the Southeast Asian economies. This is also possible in the current situation because the parties concerned have been convinced that it is necessary after what has happened. The consequence of this is that the rotten apples and old structures will disappear, thus creating opportunities for young, dynamic businesses in the region and for those further away. Although foreign investors are still cautious about making commitments in Asia, this fear is unjustified, at least as far as some countries are concerned.

Hommen looks at the Asia crisis from a positive angle: in the sense that Philips has absorbed the blows reasonably well on account of a sound financial policy and because the economies in question are once again cleaned out and therefore an excellent territory for business endeavours. Philips has therefore taken advantage of the crisis in order

9

to develop new co-operation and make new acquisitions. In addition, Philips has managed to keep its market share in Asia intact. According to Hommen, the crisis is in part the consequence of the open-handed policy of Western banks, which ultimately had to result in calamities.

With regard to the position of the European Investment Bank, De Korte notes that while the ECB is the monetary authority, EIB is the principal banker for longer term financing operations. De Korte's opinion is that the EIB, in this sense, operates as a private institution in that it strives for maximum efficiency. The operations performed by the bank also generate a surplus, which is necessary to safeguard continuity. The most important focus of the EIB's activities has always been to strive for a balanced economic situation within the EU. A very important part of this is financing projects that improve the economic situation in countries which will shortly be gaining entry into the EU. For example, the EIB has acted as a large-scale financier of projects in Greece, Spain and Portugal. In the 'Europe of the Six' the focus was on activities in the south of Italy. Nowadays, the most important areas for the EIB are the Eastern European countries that have been nominated for entry to the EU. In this context, the Board of Governors has approved an increase in the EIB's subscribed capital from 62 billion to 100 billion euro. As a consequence, the credit ceiling has been raised to 250 billion euro. This capital is very necessary in order to meet the needs of these countries in the pre-accession phase.

It is interesting to note that some smaller countries now have to pay more interest for the euro capital market than in the past for the local market. This is because they are relatively small players in the market. The same applies to the EIB's borrowing with its triple-A status compared to the borrowing capacity of the German government, which also has a triple-A status, but a much greater borrowing volume and thus pays lower rates.

Other developments

Euro

The euro is considered an important development by the majority of our 15 experts. The manner in which the currency has developed to date is seen as rather disappointing, however. Mr. Zalm, the Dutch Minister of Finance, is of the opinion that the euro must certainly be viewed as a strong currency in the long term. In international terms, the euro as a currency is now clearly weaker than the dollar. As this book goes to press the euro has reached an all-time low. Because of this, the political position of Europe with respect to the US has been undermined. No further economic integration can take place, therefore, without there being evidence of further political integration at the same time. The reason for the weakness of the euro lies in the fact that the German economy (the engine of the European economy) is underperforming and that policy has yielded too much to political pressure from certain European countries. The content of the Treaty of Maastricht must not be discussed, and it must be executed in the manner stated. The strength of the euro is linked irrevocably to the strength of the German economy. For there to be a strong currency, therefore, the German economy will have to recover.

Internationalisation

When discussing internationalisation, Van den Goorbergh states that the focus of many consortia is on the Benelux. He believes, however, that collaboration with German and French institutions is far more important in the European context. He warns, in particular, that account should be taken of the fact that the Netherlands is far more dependent on foreign (German and French) partners than these countries are on the Netherlands. A significant problem in this context is that – for a number of reasons – it is very difficult to gain access to the German market.

Experimental Economics

Also interesting is the comment on 'experimental economics' in the interview with Bilderbeek and Swagerman. To date, within strategic finance, insufficient attention has been paid to this topic. Insight into new areas can be obtained by means of 'game theory' and experiments. What comes to mind, in particular, are the auctions held on the Internet. In future, such auctions will be increasingly common.

Behavioural Finance

Benartzi devotes attention to the mysteries related to behavioural finance. If investors were to reason on the basis of the equity premium concept – from which it appears that securities have produced a much better yield over the last century – than, for example, bonds with a low risk, they would be prepared to take much greater risks. Benartzi explains this phenomenon as the irrational tendency, the investor's myopic loss aversion, to weigh losses twice as heavily as gains. The result is a shortsighted approach. An investor will often opt for a low yield bond rather than for a more risky investment, which gives a far better return. Fluctuations do occur in the return on investment, however. The downward trend that can occur causes the investor so many problems from a moral point of view that he decides against such an investment. This myopic behaviour is also due to the fact that the investor has the tendency to constantly count his money. This means that the incidental losses weigh so heavily that the investor assumes risk-avoidance behaviour.

The accountant

The persons interviewed also expressed ideas concerning the role of the accountant in the light of the outlined developments. Traas suggested that in future a new type of financial manager will be needed: one who knows the market and the product and contributes to the ideas of the company. At Philips, this is becoming possible by means of the 'knowledge bank', from which the finance manager can extract information from the accumulated know-how of the organisation. Hommen pleads similarly that the new man is no longer the traditional accountant who views events only after they have happened and certifies the financial statements, but rather someone who is actively engaged in company policymaking.

Meijer believes that the accountant must continue to make his contribution in the field of providing management information. Business is snapping up people with this expertise. The audit of financial statements has to a great extent become a commodity. By providing scarce expertise in the field of management information, the accountant can fulfil a very important role.

In conclusion

What does Strategic Finance mean for the accountant? It signifies that the accountant is aware of the developments in the socio-economic field. These changes are having repercussions on professional activities. One of the tasks of VERA, as a provider of continuing professional education for accountants, is to signal new developments. Our hope is that this publication will make a contribution in this respect.

Luc Keuleneer
Dirk Swagerman
Willem Verhoog

1. New developments in valuation

In conversation with Professor T.E. Copeland

One of the most eminent authorities in the field of valuation is Tom Copeland, not least because of the fact that he is the co-author of the standard work in the field of valuation, i.e. the well-known valuation book that will be appearing in its third edition in the spring of 2000. Professor Copeland is the most appropriate person to ask which subjects are currently under discussion in the field of finance and financing. Are fundamental changes taking place or are the developments merely a temporary fad? The developments we are thinking about in this respect are value-based management, corporate governance, discussions about the basic valuation model, the modification of discounted cash flow model and the modification of the capital costs for smaller companies, as well as the separation of elements of financial risk

Prof. T.E. Copeland

and business risk in order to give them a separate valuation. Professor Tom Copeland is also the man who can best judge whether new valuation theories, such as the application of option theory on valuation and other financial decisions, will continue to be a subject that is confined to financial scientists or whether there is a possibility that they will break through to the everyday life of financial management. These are subjects that will be discussed with Professor Copeland.

Could you please say a little about your background?

Copeland: 'I gained a Bachelors' degree in economics from the John Hopkins University in Baltimore in 1968, an MBA from Wharton in 1969 and a PhD from the University of Pennsylvania in 1973. Between 1973 and 1987, I was a faculty member at UCLA's Anderson graduate school of management where I became a full professor and chairman of the department. Between 1987 and 1998, I was a partner at McKinsey

& Co. in New York, where I was head of the corporate finance practice and since July 1998 I have been at Monitor, where I am a partner and also head of the corporate finance practice here. In addition, between 1988 and 1998 I was also adjunct professor at New York University and I have just been appointed adjunct professor at MIT where I will be teaching a course on financial engineering this coming winter.'

Why should accountants use the discounted cash flow method for valuation purposes?

Copeland: 'The first thing is to understand that the discounted cash flow valuation method is an entity or an enterprise approach where the cash flows from all sources of capital are valued and then one subtracts the value of debt to get the value of equity. The dividend discount model is an approach that is very similar in spirit. What it does is it takes the free cash flows to the shareholders, discounts them at the cost of equity and in fact one gets the same answer as with the enterprise approach.

There is an important additional consideration which is that both the discounted cash flow method and the dividend method are used to forecast the future cash flows, while the intrinsic value method uses historical information. Taking the book value of equity as an example, this has little to do with the market value of the equity and the ratio of market value to book value is rarely equal to one. There are in fact many companies that have negative intrinsic value if one is using the book value of equity as a measure. Book value is therefore not highly correlated with the market value of the company or the market value of the equity.'

What is really new about value based management compared to methods used in the past?

Copeland: 'Value based management should first be defined. The general idea is to find measures of performance at the company level or the business unit level which are highly correlated with the changes in the value of the company, in other words with the total return to shareholders. In an ideal world, if you had measures of performance that were highly correlated with the total return to shareholders then you could link your actions on a daily basis in a very direct manner to the impact on the shareholders of the company. That has proved to be a very illusive ideal so I should mention three different approaches to value based management. The approach that has been very popular in recent years is an approach that has been developed by Stern Stewart from a New York company called EVA (Economic Value Added). The idea is to take the company's return on invested capital and compare it with the weighted average cost of capital for the company. The spread between those two numbers is multiplied by the amount of invested capital to come up with an economic value added figure. In my own publications I call this "economic profit" in honour of Lord Alfred Marshall who first wrote about the subject in 1896. Recent research that I have conducted shows that the correlation between economic profit and the total return to shareholders or between economic value added and the total return to shareholders indicate is very low, 5% or less. Furthermore, the change in economic profit or the change in economic value added when correlated to total return to shareholders also has very low correlation. The reason for this leads to a second definition of value based management, which I think is better than the first. The basic idea of this definition is that management should be looking at the difference between the return on invested capital they actually earn and the return on invested capital that the market expects them to earn. This is very different to comparing the return on invested capital to the weighted average cost of capital. To give an example, in October 1997 one of the world's most profitable companies, Intel, announced that its earnings were up 19% compared to the year before. So Intel has very positive economic profit. Furthermore, with the increase in earnings the change in economic profit was positive, but in response to the announcement Intel stocks fell in price by 6%. The reason for this was very simple. It was reported in the newspapers that the reason was that the analysts had expected Intel to announce an increase of roughly 23% or 24% and, although earnings were up 20%, they was not up as much as the market had expected. So the total return to shareholders was negative on the announcement. Incidentally, in the third edition of my book on valuation there will be a lot of material on this particular point because when you are talking about the existing assets or core assets of a business, you certainly have to earn more than the market expects. Even where privately-held or family-owned businesses are concerned you still have to earn more than is expected in order to create wealth for the owners. During the last year or two I have come to the conclusion that this second definition of value based management is much more highly correlated with the total return to shareholders. In fact, I have just completed some preliminary research which indicates that the correlations are about 30% to 35% and are statistically significant.'

How do you determine the market expectations for the return on invested capital?

Copeland: 'There are two databases available in the US which contain analysts' forecasts. One of them is called ZACKS and the other is called IBES. These databases go back at least ten years and record the expectations of analysts on a weekly basis. They are representative of the markets' expectations of companies' performance, but they could probably do a better job. I would be happier if they not only captured expectations of earnings, but also of capital expenditures. They could, for instance, make a rough estimate of free cash flows, but the results are far superior to looking at the relationship between economic value added or the change in economic value added and the total return to shareholders. Managers often ask me how they can know what the market expects. There are two or three ways to respond to this. It is possible to see the historical performance of a company by looking at the business units of a company or even the company as a whole. For example, Coca-Cola is a company that has a return on invested capital in excess of 50% year after year. In order for the company to have a high return to shareholders, certainly higher than expected return, they have to earn more than 50% and not just more than 10% which is their cost of capital. If they were to earn only 30% this would be disastrous for their stock price even though they are earning more than their cost of capital. This brings me to my third point which is that, in my opinion, the best measure for performance is to look at the discounted cash flow model of a company. The comparison of the economic profits relative to the expectations of economic profit is a one period measure, while the discounted cash flows attempt to look at the performance of the company over many time periods into the future. I have found that when I correlate the discounted cash flow estimates of the value of a company with the actual market value of that company I get correlations of 80% and above.'

Can you tell us something about your experience with the practical use of value based management? What are the main practical aspects?

Copeland: 'I think there are three things. First of all, choose the right measure of performance. Secondly, create the right mindset in your management team and thirdly, implement for impact. Of course all three things work together. We have already talked about different measures so there is no need to go into that again, except perhaps why it is important not to use some of the traditional measures. For example, if you use earnings per share or the gross earnings per share you completely ignore any information about balance sheet management. Consequently, companies that focus on earnings are relatively inefficient in the way that they manage their balance sheet. It actually does make a difference whether you generate one dollar of earnings with one dollar of capital or generate the same dollar of earnings with 50 cents of capital. Other companies use return on invested capital or return on assets employed or return on net assets; there are many definitions of the same thing. What I have found is that those measures are better because the income statement information is the numerator and invested capital is the denominator. This is balance sheet information so it represents an improvement over earnings, but unfortunately if you try to maximise the return on invested capital you tend to harvest your business. The easiest thing to do is to let your invested capital base depreciate in order to increase your return on invested capital and after a while you find that you are not competitive. So that is not a particularly good measure either. Some of the traditional measures fail for the reasons that I have mentioned. In my opinion, the best value based management systems have three levels of measurement. At the corporate level and at the business unit level where you have forecasts of income statements and balance sheet, discounted cash flow is a very good tool. For one period performance measurement the difference between actual and economic profit and expected economic profit is probably the best measure. At the plant level where you don't have income statements and balance sheets, value drivers are probably the best way of measuring performance. These value drivers include things like defect rates or on-time delivery or the product mix or, in banking, the creditworthiness of the ledgers. That's all I have to say about choosing the right measure.

The next thing is the whole behavioural science issue. I have seen a lot of value based management programmes fail because the top management was enthusiastic, but the line managers could not understand why they should implement or why they should care. To change the mindset of an entire organisation you need three things. You need the support of top management, you need training so that you can make better decisions and finally you need to change compensation practices so that individual incentives are more closely aligned with the performance measurement being implemented.'

To start such a process do you immediately have to include all levels in the company or do you have to work level by level?
Copeland: 'I think that depends upon the company. I have seen situations where a business unit within a company decides that it wants

to try value based management and does this on its own initiative. If it is successful the process migrates to other business units and then eventually to headquarters. I have also seen other situations where headquarters have tried to force the new measure down everyone's throat and there is a rebellion. At one large company where I implemented value based management, the headquarters and the business units were supportive, but the division level managers were actually neutral or negative. The company therefore implemented at the headquarters first and the business units second. The division then had to go along as a result. Other companies try to roll out the system throughout the entire company at a single stroke. Some companies prefer to experiment and choose one or two businesses and try it there and see what happens.'

If you were asked to provide advice, what would you recommend as the best practice?

Copeland: 'I think the most important thing is to try to have real impact. Managers are very practical people and they will want to see decisions made better. They will support the system if it can generate new ideas that are better than those produced by the older decisions. Let me give you an example to illustrate what I mean. At one company I was sitting in the office of the manager of a major business unit when we were interrupted by an important phone call from the president of the company. After the manager had answered the call he turned to me and said: "That was the fourth quarter earnings call. The company as a whole is expected to fall short of its earnings expectations and the president wants my business unit to come up with more earnings." I asked him what he would do. He replied: "I can actually deliver the earnings, but I will have to cut back on my advertising programmes for the rest of the quarter. That will deliver this year's earnings but it will make business that much more difficult next year. I know it's the wrong thing to do in the long term, but the president has asked for more earnings and my bonus depends on more earnings and therefore I will do it." He said that the reason he supported the value based management system was that it has a multi-period perspective and prevented them from doing such silly things. The reason he was supportive was that he believed that the new value based management approach would prevent what he considered to be self-destructive behaviour.'

But is this self-destructive behaviour so important in the market at the moment? Is it not the case that financial markets and financial analysts are pushing towards short-term thinking in the boardrooms?

Copeland: 'I don't think there is any definitive answer to that, but again I can refer to our research because we get analyst forecasts not only on this year's earnings but earnings two years ahead, and then we also get long-term forecasts. Interestingly enough, the forecasts that are two years ahead and long-term forecasts have a higher weight in their relationship to total return to shareholders this year than this year's forecast does. Although it does not answer the question, it does indicate to me that the analysts not only look at this year's earnings, but they look at next year's earnings and long-term earnings as well. Therefore, the market does actually seem to put high weight on the longer-term estimates.'

Are you in favour of more regulation of financial markets to guarantee both information flows and longer term thinking?

Copeland: 'If analysts and investors demand better information about companies in order to value them why wouldn't the companies supply that information. My personal point of view is that some broad regulations help create the market place for information and help it to work more efficiently. In my opinion, rules that aim to prevent insider trading actually help the market.'

Is the theoretical basis for maximising shareholder value the same inside and outside the US and is the valuation approach outside the US just a copy of the US approach?

Copeland: 'At one level, mainly the official level, there certainly are differences. In Germany, for example, I know that there is an official government approach to valuation that is different from the discounted cash flow approach, although in a recent revision of the government regulations the two are coming closer together but are still not perfectly aligned. On the other hand, I believe the valuation approach that is written about in my book is used as the primary valuation approach throughout the world. The ideas in the book are not original, but I would say the scientific method could be applied to a discipline like valuation. People have tried different approaches to different methodologies for valuing companies over the centuries and the approach that I write about has stood the test of time better than any other approach. Articles on the subject have been published in leading journals. One that was published a few years ago by Kaplan and Ruback (Journal of Finance, 1996), which examined the discounted cash flows against valuation multiples, found that discounted cash flows did better statistically. A surviving methodology would seem to be the one that best explains the reality that we observe and so far the survivor seems to be the discounted cash flow valuation method, at least where large firms are concerned.

The history of discounted cash flow evaluation goes back to the 1930's and the work by Modigliani and Miller in the late 1950's introduced a more modern approach to the subject. They were followed by many other scholars, including Malkieland then Alfred Rappaport who took the formula approach and turned it into a spreadsheet approach which is used by most people these days. I have done valuations in 30 or 40 different countries and the discounted cash flow approach works equally well in Japan and in Germany and in the US and in Brazil.'

Do you think there is a relationship between corporate governance and the value of the firm? In your opinion, what are the 'best practices in corporate governance'?

Copeland: 'First of all, the valuation will value any company the way it is with its current governance. The question is whether you can change the value of a company if you change its governance. There is some academic literature that seems to indicate that there is a relationship. All of the evidence is based on data from the US, however, so it is quite limited in its implications for other countries. Nevertheless, there is evidence that when the board of directors of a company changes and introduces more outsiders the market reacts favourably to that announcement. There are also indications that stock prices go up when a company announces changes in compensation from a strict salary and bonus to stock options or stock grants. There are two explanations for this. One is that a better alignment between the management team and the shareholder's objective causes the shareholders to value the company more highly. It could also mean that the management team believes that the company is going to do better in the future and that the shareholders use the options plan as a signal that the company will do better in the future. So the cause and effect for the two explanations are different.

Corporate governance in every country is inextricably linked with the political environment and the social environment within which corporations operate. I actually think that the most important starting point is to talk about capital and labour mobility within the country, although I don't know of any evidence that shows that changes in corporate governance influence the structure of capital and labour mobility. I can give you an example from my own personal experience.

The government of a particular country was privatising a government-owned bank. It was put up for sale and I represented one of the companies that was potentially going to bid for the bank. When you looked at the bank you found out that it was very inefficient, the deposits per employee were about half the deposits per employee for competing banks in the same country. You would think that a change in governance, i.e. a change in ownership from government ownership to private ownership, would create a lot of efficiency in the bank and we thought so too until at the end of one week of looking at it we were reminded that in this particular country if you lay off an employee you must pay them four year's income regardless of how long they had been working for the company. Therefore, you will not be surprised when I tell you that labour mobility in this country was very low and unemployment was very high. Therefore, the change in corporate governance (in this case the privatisation of the bank) that was proposed as a solution actually never took place because of this labour law. All the potential private owners except one withdrew from bidding and the one bid was so low that the government rejected it. The government bank is still there, it is still inefficient, labour mobility is still low and corporate governance can't solve the problem. I don't know of any studies that have been able to separate corporate governance from the entire fabric of society.'

It is common practice is to use the weighted average cost of capital (WACC) as discount rate, but a new approach is emerging: the APV (adjusted present value), where a discount rate excluding the financial risk is used. Are you in favour of this approach for valuations and/or investment analysis?

Copeland: 'First of all, the APV approach and the discounted cash flow approach are mathematically identical. Therefore, the only differences between the approaches are practical ones. I have an issue with applying the APV approach in situations where there is relatively high leverage and yet these are exactly the situations where it is claimed that the APV approach does better. What you have to do to apply the APV approach is to first of all observe comparable companies to get an estimate of their cost of equity which is a leveraged cost of equity. You then have to use some approach, usually the capital asset pricing model (CAPM), to unleverage the observed levered equity in order to produce an unlevered equity estimate. The operating free cash flows of the company are then discounted at that unleveraged cost of equity to get an estimate of the value of the company if it has no debt. The present value of the debt tax shield is then added to this; the tax rate is multiplied by the interest payments and then discounted at the cost of debt. The advocates of the APV approach focus on the second part of that equation. They say it is much easier in higher leverage situations to estimate the way in which the interest tax shield will change over time and then to discount it at the cost of debt. What I am focusing on is the first term, i.e. the operating cash flows divided by the unlevered cost of the equity. What I wanted to point out is that in order to estimate the unlevered cost of equity in higher leverage situations you have to make an assumption that is not valid. If you look at a comparable company that is highly leveraged and use the formula for unleveraging the cost of equity, the figure that is used assumes that the cost of debt for that company is equal to the risk free rate. That is simply not a valid assumption and therefore the estimates of the unlevered cost of equity are biased. I didn't see anything in the Harvard Business Review article that told me how to correct for that bias. I do have some proprietary ways of correcting for that bias but the Harvard Business Review article focused entirely on the advantages of the second term and didn't even mention the disadvantages of the first term. If I thought that the APV approach was better I would be using it, but frankly I find it more cumbersome.'

A lot of research is being performed into the cost of equity and the capital asset pricing model (CAPM). Is the CAPM an adequate method for estimating the cost of equity? What is your opinion about adding a 'small firm premium' to the CAPM as some of the larger accounting firms do?

Copeland: 'My opinion is that there is nothing conclusive yet. The article that was written by Fama & French in 1992 started a careful re-examination of the problem because their conclusion was that, after carefully controlling for the size of the company and the book to market ratio, they found no evidence that these added anything to explaining the cost of equity or the cross-sectional differences in the rates of return on equities. There has been some subsequent work that has been somewhat critical of Fama and French. First of all, it has been pointed out that when they did their work they had to use two databases instead of one. Traditionally, research in this area has used the CRSP (Chicago Research & Securities Price) database, which is a good database because no company ever leaves the database. Once a company is listed it is given a permanent number and even if the company goes bankrupt the permanent number remains on the tape indicating that the company has once been there.

They added to the sample by going to Compustat, which had extended its database by adding a lot of small firms. When it did so it created a bias in the data because the small firms that were added were those from the total set of small firms that had survived up to that point in time. So implicitly, when you combine the two databases the rates of return on the smaller firms in the database are higher than they otherwise would be without the survivorship by its problem. It is believed that this induces the small firm effect that was found in Fama & French.

There is a very nice paper by Kothari Shanken & Sloan that clearly illustrates the problems in Fama & French and when other authors redo the work they find that beta is in fact once again significant in explaining the cross-sectional differences in returns. You find that people are taking the Fama & French result and ignoring later evidence and coming to the conclusion, for example, that a risk premium be added to small firms. My suggestion is that they look at all the evidence and not just some of the evidence. I have read the literature very carefully and I would say that the jury is still out on the applicability of the capital asset pricing model. We still use the capital asset pricing model framework, but we have changed the way that the market risk premium is estimated. Remember that the market risk premium is the difference between the expected return on the market and the risk-free rate and that is what you multiply with the beta in order to add a risk premium to the risk-free rate to get the cost of equity. In the second edition of my book we use the long-term geometric average return on the market to estimate the market risk premium. In the third edition we have changed to the long-term arithmetic average which is a higher number. We are also aware of the fact that there is undoubtedly survivorship bias in using the New York stock exchange index. When we subtract the survivorship bias from the long-term arithmetic US exchange return we get a market risk premium in the 5-6% range.'

Can you explain the link between the concepts of option theory and valuation? Is option theory useful in practice and if so, how do you aim to convince managers that it is useful?

Copeland: 'Real options are an emerging field of financial engineering that in my opinion will completely replace net present value in the next 10 years. The reason is that net present value is a flawed model for evaluating projects.

A typical example of a net present value problem would be a project that is expected to last 10 years; you have forecasts of the expected growth of revenues and the expected costs, so that allows you to figure out the expected free cash flows net of the working capital and capital expenditures. You then discount those free cash flows and the weighted average cost of capital and subtract the initial capital investment. If the resulting number is greater than zero, the project is said to have a positive net present value and so you should accept it. The problem is that managers who experience these decisions know that that approach is full of implied assumptions that are rigid or even wrong. For example, if you start a project and it turns out to be going badly, it will not last ten years but will be either abandoned or scaled down. Furthermore, if it is a successful project its life will either be extended or it will be scaled up. Finally, no one says that the initial investment has to take place right now, it could take place next year or the year after, which is a deferral option. All managers know that there are abandonment options, extension options, contraction options, expansion options and deferral options in every project. Experienced managers have all been in situations where they have taken the net present value numbers and basically thrown them away, because their intuition told them that flexibility will add value to the project. If you frame the issue in that way you therefore begin to realise that net present value is very limited.

If the net present value is so limited, why is it being used so much? The reason is that there are many situations where the difference between the net present value answer and the real options answer is quite small. There are situations where the net present value is very high, for example if there is no need to have the flexibility of shutting the project down, as you will never exercise that option. Similarly, if a project has a huge negative net present value, no amount of flexibility provided by options will save it. But interestingly enough, companies are turning to experts and real options to help them to think through problems in the case of the projects that have a net present value close to zero, the ones in the grey area, where you can get differences between real options valuation and net present value which are in the order of 100%. Perhaps only one in ten projects that fall into that category, but I'll give you some examples where real options should be used.

The decision facing Airbus and Boeing about whether or not to build a 500-600-seat passenger aircraft is in a grey area and represents a huge investment of $10 billion and 10 years of development for either company. Other examples in the transportation area are Taiwan Rapid Rail or Railtrack in the UK. These are $10-20 billion investments that will take 20-30 years to finish and are also in the grey area.

During the last five years, people have started to realise that you can't use Black & Scholes or in fact any other closed form solution for a real options problems. You really have to use a lattice approach, the simplest example of which is the binomial tree. Research and development programme investments are usually multi-phased so to solve problems you need to build a decision tree and a lattice behind it. One of the advantages of this approach is that you really only need to be able to point to one branch in the lattice at a time and explain to a manager how that branch is priced. I predict that over the next ten years you will see more and more applications of real options in major project decisions. Academics are increasingly coming to the point of view that this is the only way to teach investment decisions and that net present value is a special case of real options.

Scientific methods have been applied to explaining the prices that we observe in the market place. If the discounted cash flow method did not work well, we would be using some other method. However, it does explain reality very well. Financial markets must have proper information about companies in order to put proper values on them. This is why the shareholders of a company require monitoring and financial statements. It is not the government, but the shareholders that require financial statements. If there were no regulations we would therefore still have financial statements. The quality of the information is aided by a certain amount of standardisation imposed by regulations requiring that information be released. None of what we have talked about can work very well unless the market has had good information. What we are seeing around the world is that more and more markets are opening up and information is flowing better and this means that the tools of modern corporate finance can be used much more effectively.

In my opinion, regulations can hurt as well as help. When governments decide to defend currencies or restrict flows, the free markets cannot work. On the other hand, governments do help to some extent by imposing standardised requirements. I would like to see more open markets where individuals can be confident that when they make a trade the settlement of the trade will take place in an orderly fashion and that the transaction is secure.'

In your opinion, what will be the hot topics in finance in the coming ten years?

Copeland: 'I think that international finance will be a clear area of development. I think that real options will develop. Hot topics will continue to be the intelligent use of derivatives and the entire debate about the capital asset pricing model and the arbitrage pricing model and competing models. In addition, the relationship between the organisation of decision makers and the ability to create value will be a hot topic that will find its expression in the form of corporate governance issues and value based management and performance measurement.'

2A Strategy and finance: complementary terms?

In conversation with Professor L.M.F.J. Keuleneer and Mr. L. Van Steenberge

The theme of this book is 'Strategic Finance' which may call up all sorts of associations with 'struggle' and the solving of conflict, or with sporting contests in which winning a victory and thus undying esteem (and naturally material gain) are the main objectives. The word 'strategy' has its origins in warfare and then particularly in the making and implementation of plans for large-scale military exercises. The word is also frequently used in the business world. Mergers, acquisitions, raiding techniques, the elimination of the competition, hegemony or defence mechanisms are all metaphors derived from military strategy. The second term in the title of this book relates to the financing and points directly to the ambiguity of the title: financing at the strategic level and financing of a strategy. After all, with money resources can be obtained to realise particular objectives. Which ends? How much money? Which resources? Which sources? How is it to be obtained? Each decision requires new decisions. That is precisely what strategy entails. And the question how many advance moves the 'chess players' in this power game should consider, is difficult to answer. After all, this depends upon their strategy.

Prof. L.M.F.J. Keuleneer

Mr. L. Van Steenberge

How can strategic decisions be theoretically underpinned? Which instruments are available to prepare and perform strategic analyses? How should strategic analyses be translated in terms of value? How can one evaluate whether a particular strategy creates value or even destroys it? These and other questions were presented to Professor Luc Keuleneer (whose curriculum vitae is included at the end of this book; page 192) and Mr. Leo Van Steenberge, Senior Partner at Deloitte & Touche in Brussels. Both work with the Value Based Management model and the associated balanced scorecard.

Can a manager be compared to a strategist?

Prof. Keuleneer: 'Comparisons don't hold water by definition. One of the most important tasks of the management of a company is providing direction for a company's future developments. The comparison between a ship, or the company, the captain, or the management and the position being determined is therefore often made for good reason. In other words, after the planning comes the implementation. It is also about really bringing about the desired developments and monitoring the results. External developments that suddenly occur must also be taken into account so that it is possible to set or change course in good time. But first and foremost, there must be a vision of the future – of the sector and of the direction that the company will take – before an organisation enters a new phase.'

It is possible to be trained as a captain, and as a manager, but is a diploma a guarantee of professional skills?

Mr. Van Steenberge: 'In principle there are particular professional training courses for most professions, but some activities require specific talents. Those lacking artistic talents will probably never become a good painter, singer or actor. Those who do have the talents do well to develop them properly by means of vocational training. This is no different for managers. But what distinguishes an ordinary manager from a good manager? What makes a good manager into an excellent manager? When does excellent become brilliant? And when is a manager considered to be highly gifted? These questions are usually academic, but are sometimes very specific and topical, particularly when a company is balancing on the edge and very important decisions must be taken very quickly. You see this in situations in which a particular management has failed and must be replaced by a crisis management team.

A good manager distinguishes himself from less talented colleagues by his creativity and clear vision. These properties lead to a strategy that gives the company a lead over the competition. Obviously, the strategy must be practicable. The set targets must be within reach or otherwise brought within reach. That is what it's about: taking action at all levels in the organisation, realising formulated objectives with the creation of value as the final goal. This is a dynamic process. Strategy – and even the lack of it – always exercises a direct influence on the financial performance of a company and thus on the creation of value for the shareholders.'

Does the shareholder have sufficient insight into the strategy that 'his' company has developed?

Prof. Keuleneer: 'No, indeed many companies don't have that either. For the sake of convenience let us start with two companies A and B that achieve the same results, but do this on the basis of different strategies. A consciously takes risks, B avoids them. I am also assuming that both companies have the same turnover, make the same purchases, have the same gross margin, the same costs and the same profit. The difference is that A has more fixed assets, more long-term liabilities and higher reserves. As a result, B has a higher return on assets than A, but has the risk-averse company B thereby done any better than the risk-taking company A? No, because I must first know which strategy the two companies have pursued in the field of research and development, marketing, training, investment and so on. Since company A has invested more in assets than B, it will probably be able to realise higher cash flows in the future than B. To put it briefly, it is vitally important to situate the company within its environmental parameters and to understand its strategy in order to determine how valuable it is.'

What are the typical instruments for strategic analysis?

Mr. Van Steenberge: 'During the past few years, a number of instruments have been developed to perform strategic analyses faster and more efficiently. These include: the value chain and value system, the environmental analysis of Michael Porter and the growth share matrix of the Boston Consulting Group (BCG).

To start with the value chain and value system: a company maintains a relationship with a large number of stakeholders of whom providers of capital, employees, customers and suppliers have a direct interest in the organisation. Governments, social groupings and competitors have indirect and often conflicting interests in the company.

Parties with a direct interest form part of the company's value chain.

Parties with an indirect interest form no part of this, but certainly have an influence on the objectives and ambitions. To a great extent, they determine the preconditions and control the value chain. Each interested party, direct or indirect, demands or expects a particular result from the company. The shareholder, for instance, is the owner and provider of risk-bearing capital and in return demands a minimum return on his invested capital. The employees provide their labour and do their best (in theory) to realise an optimum result with the resources placed at their disposal. They expect continuity in their employment and a reasonable remuneration for their share in the company's achievements. And suppliers and customers also have similar reciprocal expectations. The result of the strategy should therefore be that the level and quality of the results are also maintained over the longer period. This determines the shareholder value.'

Prof. Keuleneer: 'Porter's environmental analysis is dominated by the intensity of the competition in a particular line of business. The competition depends upon five factors. The American investment analyst M. Porter has elaborated on these in his Five Forces Model. The first factor that determines the level of competition is the threat of new entrants. The developments in the IT sector can be given as an example. The second factor is the negotiating position of the supplier. In the IT sector, a few large suppliers of processors have, for instance, been running the show for years. The third factor is the position of the customers. If the market is saturated, the producer becomes more dependent upon its customers, for instance. The fourth factor is the rivalry between existing companies. Here as well, the IT sector has also shown persuasive examples of this. The fifth and final factor is the threat of substitute products and/or services. A typewriter manufacturer that thirty or forty years ago still thought it faced a bright future will probably now no longer exist.

If you want to develop an efficient competitive strategy these days, you must make a clear analysis of these five factors. So what is "my" sector doing here? You must subsequently establish the strong and weak points of your company with respect to these five factors. This is done on the basis of SWOT analysis, the strength/weakness analysis.

The negotiating position with respect to suppliers and customers – actually also with respect to other parties on other markets, such as labour market and capital market for instance – is obviously of vital importance for the competitive position of the company. If the negotiating positions of the other parties become too strong, this works against the company when negotiations take place about prices and fees. The selection of the suppliers and customers is therefore an important strategic choice for a company.

New entrants or substitute products or services also affect the existing balance. You must therefore investigate how unique the knowledge, experience and assets of your company are. How high are the obstacles that the new competitors must take? Examples include investments, learning curve effects and the like. How unique are the company's products? Are they available in sufficient quantities? Are there any acceptable substitutes available?

In other words, the company must develop a strategy, which creates a market position, from where attacks – another term from the military world – by the competition can be intercepted and factors that have a negative influence on the market position can be controlled.'

You referred to the growth share matrix as a third instrument for performing strategic analyses. What does this entail?

Mr. Van Steenberge: 'It is an instrument for performing strategic analyses more quickly and more efficiently. This matrix was developed by the Boston Consulting Group (BCG) and presents the portfolio of the stages of life of a company's products. The market growth rate is compared against the relative market share.

The stage of life in which a product or business find itself determines the strategies that a company must develop. The BCG distinguishes four qualifications for companies: stars, question marks, cash cows and dogs.

The "stars" try to capture the greatest possible market share in an expanding market. These companies invest a lot of their own funds in order to strengthen market position. Considerable emphasis is placed on marketing.

The "question marks" are companies that try to gain an ever-increasing market share by investing substantial amounts. They grow rapidly and, on account of the big investments, the growth must mainly be financed with external capital.

The "cash cows" have reached a saturation stage and turn to their record of service and market share in order to realise high profits. In addition, they invest little.

The "dogs" lose market share and are also unable to grow any longer. In order to realise profits they must cut costs. These companies have to focus mainly on their core business and must try and divest or spin-off non-growth departments.'

When and where does Value Based Management (VBM) come into the picture in the business strategy?

Prof. Keuleneer: 'With the aid of the instruments referred to, a strategy must be developed which ensures that the ability of the company to generate cash flows is maximised. As soon as this strategy is formulated, shareholder value is created; or destroyed, that is also possible of course. This explains why the announcement of a change in business strategy often has an effect on the share price, while there are not necessarily any changes in the actual activities and commercial operations.

If the company wants to be able to optimally focus its objectives and activities on the creation of value, there should be a system that facilitates the management, measurement and evaluation of value. The system that is claimed to do this is Value Based Management or VBM.

VBM is a strategic financial decision-making and management model. It focuses on maximising the enterprise value in the medium to long term. With the aid of VBM it is possible to define the strategic choices, which should increase the value of the company in the long term. With VBM the continuity of the company can be guaranteed in the long term by creating and maximising shareholder value.'

Mr. Van Steenberge: 'The success of a company is realised on the commercial market. The company must supply products and services that the market demands with a good price/quality ratio. To access the commercial market, capital is required. This is provided by the capital market in the form of internal and external capital. The providers of capital demand compensation in the form of added value, interest or dividend, among other things for taking risk and deferring consumption. The company must therefore be able to generate sufficient funds on the commercial market – that is the operational cash flow – in order to meet the demands of the providers of capital. That is the free cash flow.

A company is only successful and only creates value if it generates more funds than the providers of capital expect or, in other words, if the financial performance – that is called the Net Operating Profit After Taxes – is better in the long term than the return which the providers of internal and external capital expect on their invested capital. This is referred to as the Weighted Average Cost of Capital or WACC. Naturally, account is taken of the risk profile of the company's activities.'

How is the shareholder value network set up in a company?

Prof. Keuleneer: 'In the case of VBM, the level of the value creation in a particular strategy is more specifically determined by the so-called "value drivers". These are the factors that determine the ability of the company to generate liquid assets. With the aid of these factors it is possible to calculate the existing shareholder value, as well as the shareholder value of the optimum strategy. In general, seven factors are assumed as "financial value drivers". These are: turnover growth, operational margin, investments in operating capital, investments in fixed assets, duration of the competitive advantage, the cost of capital and the effective tax rate.

The "Weighted Average Cost of Capital" (WACC) is the weighted average cost of debt and equity. The weighting used is based on the ratios of internal and external capital that the company has set as a target for the planning horizon (on the basis of the market value). The cost of the net equity consists of the risk-free return plus the systematic risk of the company (the beta) times the risk premium.

The capital structure (debt rate, stock rate) is therefore, as already stated, an important element of the WACC. In business financing, an attempt has been made, since the two Modigliani & Miller propositions from 1958, to find an answer to the question what the ideal or optimum capital structure of the company is. An important conclusion is that the optimum capital structure is a derivative of the level of debt financing. This is because of the existence of market imperfections, such as taxation and bankruptcy costs. A company is, for example, more likely to borrow money if it can claim an interest allowance. The ideal capital structure is therefore the capital structure that minimises the WACC, such that account is taken of the company's risk profile.'

The so-called value gap is a live topic. Some even see a reason for delisting companies. What do they mean?

Prof. Keuleneer: 'The value gap partly occurs when the information that (potential) investors have about the company and everything associated with it, substantially differs from the information that the management has at its disposal. This is the so-called Agency problem. This perception gap can be bridged by good communication in the first instance. This is the first step in the analysis.

A second possibility is to implement improvements in the company's performance, both at the strategic and operational level. This is the second step.

The third step of the analysis evaluates the possibilities of increasing the value of the company with the aid of acquisitions and disinvestments. Insight is sought into the extent to which justice is done to specific activities as operations of the company. In other words, are the necessary knowledge and the necessary skills optimally present?

The fourth step of the analysis attempts to optimise the capital and risk structure of the company with the aid of knowledge in the field of corporate finance and treasury management.

If you compare the current market value of the company with the value after the fourth step, you gain insight into the size and the explanatory factors of the perception gap. You can then take measures so that the company maximises its value and thus also its shareholder value.'

How should Value Based Management be implemented and measured in a company?

Mr. Van Steenberge: 'The Balanced Scorecard was developed for this purpose. During the implementation, the emphasis lies on the control of the company. The operational value drivers are actually the basis for the result indicators. The more clearly the value drivers are formulated, the easier it is to put the result measurement into effect.

It is important to select precisely those operational value-determining factors that continually require the attention of the management: these are the main result indicators. These can quickly be determined by applying the Balanced Scorecard model and by establishing the critical success factors, i.e. those factors which are of decisive importance for the success of the company. They relate to those areas that require and deserve constant attention from the management. I will mention just a few of these. The customer perspective is, for example, a critical success factor: how does the customer see the company? The internal perspective is also one: in which areas should the company improve its own performance? I can mention the innovation or learning perspective: where are improvements possible in the field of customer and operations and where can value be added? I should also mention the financial perspective: what does the company look like for its shareholders and financiers? The answers to these questions are partly subjective and partly not, but they can be measured in most cases and are certainly significant. These critical success factors are then linked to the performance indicators, such as Economic Value Added (EVA).'

Why should valuation and strategy be integrated?

Prof. Keuleneer: 'Valuation plays an important role in the strategic process. In this way the management is forced to be explicit and precise in its strategic analysis and is compelled to focus on cash flow, risks and the future. It also becomes possible to calculate value and measure the chance of success if changes occur in hypotheses; this is sensitivity analysis. Furthermore, the potential chances of succeeding or failing with a particular business portfolio receive attention. This in turn stimulates the development of a more refined strategic analysis. I should also mention the efficient allocation of resources to business units, which once again creates more value. Companies are then able to learn the real value of their business units at least as well as the investors.'

Mr. Van Steenberge: 'Some critical comments should be made in this respect. The process is complementary to a qualitative analysis of strategic foundations, but it certainly does not replace this. Therefore, it is not "or/or", but "and/and". Secondly, I would like to emphasise that creativity and strategic thinking must not be subordinated. The model can never replace human contributions. Thirdly, steps should be taken to ensure that the figures do not get in the way of strategic decisions. You cannot get away from the fact that a solution must be found for the weighing of imponderables, the immeasurable factors which often have considerable influence on the reaching and taking of decisions and on their success.

Therefore, if a company wants to value things properly, it must be possible to rationalise and evaluate its strategy. As soon as you understand why a particular decision has been reached, you are in a better position to judge the effect of different strategies. The best decision is taken, given the circumstances and information available at the moment of the decision. Only then are you able to optimise the business strategy and produce well-considered alternatives and thus maximise the shareholder value.'

Prof. Keuleneer: 'What makes the shareholder value concept unique is that it indicates what a company should strive for in order to guarantee continuity. This is partly guaranteed by the shareholder value and also by maximising the balance of the discounted future cash flows.

Value management as an integral part of the management system goes hand in hand with the development of a new strategic financial management model. But as is the case with all innovations and improvements, success depends upon acceptance by the management. Only then can the new way of thinking be anchored in the day-to-day commercial operations and in the business culture.'

2B Shareholder value and financial management

In conversation with Professor J. Bilderbeek and Mr. D.M. Swagerman MBA MBT

During the past few years, financial management has been captivated by its desire to optimise shareholder value. Most companies say that they give the shareholder priority and do their utmost best to satisfy the shareholder who was so harshly treated in the past. But is the shareholder, as perceived in the Anglo-Saxon world, really suited to other cultures, like the Western European one? Isn't it time to make some differentiation? In the Rhineland model and the Polder model, the relationship that the company should maintain with all involved stakeholders occupies centre stage. And the Polder model in particular can pride itself upon successes. Now that shareholder value is gaining in importance in continental Europe, the question arises whether matters haven't been taken a little too far. Is it necessary to introduce an Anglo-Saxon model to replace a reasonably well tried and tested Western European model? We presented these and other questions to Professor Jan Bilderbeek (Professor of Financial Management and Business Economics at the University of Twente; visiting Professor at the Hunan International Business School in Changsha, China; member of the Board of

Prof. J. Bilderbeek

Mr. D.M. Swagerman MBA MBT

37

Management of Rabobank and also member of the supervisory boards of a number of medium-sized companies) and Mr. Dirk Swagerman MBA MBT, whose curriculum vitae is included at the end of this book (page 191).

The concept of shareholder value is currently at the centre of attention. The frequently used term does have its limitations, however.

Prof. Bilderbeek: 'In my opinion, shareholder value can be regarded as a theoretical expression of a historically and culturally determined Anglo-Saxon notion about the essence of a company. This is also something that I recognise in the current discussion about "corporate governance" system in the Netherlands as well as in China. The Anglo-Saxon model is competitive and has a short-term focus and deviates from the Rhineland model (among others the Netherlands and Germany), the Latin and the Southeast Asian (Keiretsu, Chaebol) model. The latter models appear to have a more long-term focus and to be directed more towards a balanced/harmonious promotion of the interests of the various stakeholders (including, but not only the shareholders). Dutch companies that apply the concept, such as Stork for example, therefore make adjustments, such as not regarding investments in R & D as an investment in the "capital base", in order to reduce the short-term effect. The "balanced-score card" can also be seen as a response to the short-term focus. The original concept is thus apparently unsatisfactory and adjustments are made to the concept to make the best of a bad job. The fact that the concept is receiving so much attention in the Rhineland environment can perhaps be regarded as a response to the social reporting in the nineteen seventies and the environmental reporting in the nineteen eighties; in the nineteen nineties the shareholder is once again occupying centre stage, perhaps too central in the Anglo-Saxon environment in connection with the outlined "short-term" deficiency. To put it briefly, the concept, whether adjusted or not, "only" appears suitable for that environment.

As far as I am aware, there are no empirically substantiated studies available that show that the Anglo-Saxon model would produce better social and economic results than the other models. Personally, we have the impression that the opposite is true: it appears plausible that the social and economic achievements of Western European countries like Denmark, Germany, the Netherlands, Austria and Switzerland do surpass those of Australia, New Zealand, Canada, the UK and the US.

When talking about the application of the shareholder value concept, modified or not, in a non-Anglo-Saxon environment, we should realise that only part of the business community has shareholders. One-man businesses, partnerships, limited partnerships and also (sometimes large) co-operatives do not have shareholders, but do compete with businesses that do have shareholders. If the latter category is to keep up the competition, shareholders may indeed have to receive "satisfying" remuneration, but that is nevertheless quite different than "maximising the shareholder's value".

A fourth limitation in this respect relates to the fact that the "objective" calculation of the company value is only possible in the case of listed companies. This calculation is concerned with the expected free cash flows discounted from the weighted average capital cost base (the so-called "discounted free cash flows"). The cost of shareholders' equity naturally plays a role in this capital cost base, together with the so-called beta (β). For listed companies this beta is fixed "reasonably objectively" (regularly published in various newspapers), but this is not the case with companies that are not listed on the stock exchange. Where these latter companies are concerned, a beta is "estimated" on the basis of the beta of a comparable listed company. This process of additions and subtractions is subjective so that for this category of companies the original advantage of "objective" risk estimation no longer applies. Incidentally, this subjectiveness limitation does apply to listed companies that want to apply various betas internally depending upon the risk profile of the relevant divisions, business units, projects or however you wish to call the relevant entities within a company.'

What is the situation with regard to the changing function of the annual report?

Mr. Swagerman: 'The annual report is and will continue to be important! It is the information supply function of the annual report that is subject to change. This involves looking at the term "true and fair view", which an annual report must satisfy, in a different manner. The reference to the true and fair view is suffused with the statutory requirements (disclosures). A number of problems can be distinguished. The question is whether the (business) community is really interested in implementing fundamental changes in the form and the quality of the presentation. I will mention a few possible changes. A comment was already made about the relevance of market value compared to book value. Keep in mind that reporting on market value with results in late volatility in the context of presentation. The annual report does not always convey the value of the company. Just consider a high-tech company like Microsoft. The balance sheet value does not correspond at all with the market value. The market value shows the value of the company from future cash flows on the basis of the "efficient market hypothesis" and the market may make a high estimate of these future cash flows. This cannot be adequately shown by the balance sheet and you can of course ask yourself what the purpose of the balance sheet is. Whatever the case, the value of the company is not fully expressed in the annual report.

In addition, there are the intangible assets. The economy is inclined towards a service economy, which confronts us with the question how intellectual property should be valued. In a production environment it is easy to value the assets and with this type of company the intangible assets do not play such an important role. The intangible assets developed by the company itself do not appear on the balance sheet, but may nevertheless form an important part of the company's competitive power.

Another aspect is that the annual report only appears some time after the close of the financial year. The published annual report may then be superseded and no longer provide up-to-date information. Subsequent events must of course also be reported and they may certainly be important when the organisation in question is going through an extremely dynamic period. Interested parties want information about the company as it happens and shouldn't have to wait until the publication of the annual report. Currently, other sources are able to produce the required information, such as through business analysts. Finally, I would like to mention that the management is increasingly concerned with the control of a company on the basis of added value. It is increasingly important to obtain added value from the activities. This is somewhat different from placing the emphasis on realising the highest turnover.

In this connection, I would like to say something about the importance and benefit of cash-flow information. This information provides insight into what is actually received in cash, separately from the depreciation. A major part of the modern manager's actions are based on this information. We all know that the figure shown on the bottom line of the profit and loss account can be the subject of different bookkeeping opinions and thus be inadequate as the sole basis for management. But emphasising the importance of the cash flow summary is not enough; there are still a few unsolved problems. The problem of the timeliness of the information about the company must be solved. Within the current context, it should be possible to report, or provide information, more frequently. In the US, there is pressure to produce good quarterly figures. Sometimes there is a unilateral emphasis on producing favourable quarterly figures, although a company is not continually able to influence these, of course. If the reporting time will be shortened the problems of adjusting rates to a particular period will be more difficult. There is also an increasing demand for information to be provided about future developments. The annual report only provides scant information about this. The directors' report does provide forecasts for the coming year, but the value of this is limited. This also appears from the frequency with which profits warnings are given. The MD&A Report (compulsory in the US for the SEC and for an IPO on the AEX) should provide information about future developments. This can be a first step towards obtaining further prospective information in a more formalised manner.

It may be crystal-gazing, but there may be a need in the longer term to maintain a database in which organisations can dump data that can be consulted by interested parties. Information is then immediately made available to the stakeholders. This is already the case in the US for SEC companies. Large companies already work internally with a database warehouse concept whereby all information is gathered and then extracted to produce the necessary reports. This does considerably speed up the reporting time.'

A comment can be made about strategic decisions/calculations. These aspects have a different time dimension and are important for the calculation of the enterprise value.

Prof. Bilderbeek: 'The weighted average cost of capital (WACC) is a time-based variable (incorporating the future market expectations of the company in question at a particular time) and strategic decisions usually extend over a (very) long period. The distinguishing characteristic of the WACC as a time-based variable is that its level can change. This change may be the result of variations in the relative amount of shareholders' and borrowed capital over time. The result of these variations can be eliminated by not relying on the actual Debt/Equity ratio, but on the WACC associated with a so-called targeted' debt/equity ratio. The issue of the optimum capital (D/E) structure is an unsolved scientific puzzle, which means that the choice of a targeted capital structure is subjective, taking account of what is considered to be a realistic capital structure for particular business sectors during a particular period of time. Here as well, we also miss an objectivity advantage. However, in the case of a "given" (or desired) capital structure, the WACC can also change as a result of variations in the cost base of the equity and debt caused by changes in the risk profile of the company in question and/or changes in the capital markets. The consequence of this is that particular strategic investment decisions could be approved today but not tomorrow, because they exceed the WACC "hurdle rate" today but not tomorrow. In our opinion, this could hamper the investment decision-making process, so that is the reason why I am in favour of companies basing their decisions on a desired (minimum) profitability requirement in the longer term. The formulation of this profitability requirement has therefore also become a strategic decision (and so also subjective, unfortunately) and can in terms of the time involved be brought into line with the strategic planning process of a company.

The residual value has a relatively strong influence on the enterprise value to be calculated. When calculating this, the free cash flows are estimated over a particular period (usually a number of years). After this period, the company does not cease to exist; for this purpose a residual value is "estimated" which is discounted in the enterprise value and usually has a relatively strong influence on this. Of course, you can determine the effects of a number of residual value scenarios on the enterprise value that is to be calculated, although this does not in itself increase the objectivity, but it does increase the "feeling" for deviations. In my opinion, the residual value problem argues in favour of a strategically less quantifiable vision in preference to the "apparently objective" quantified financial result.

Our third consideration still has the character of a question to which I will only attempt to make a start at finding an answer. Isn't it the case that risk is counted twice? To a certain extent, that's true. The numerator contains the estimated free cash flows, while the WACC is the denominator. For many companies, the estimated free cash flows in the long term will be predominantly determined by the operational cash flows. Investment cash flows and financing cash flows must eventually have an effect on the operational cash flows. These operational cash flows are to a significant extent determined by the estimated income and expenditure resulting from the primary business processes. The balance of this estimated income and expenditure (the operational cash flows, therefore) may change over time either more strongly than the average of all other companies, about the same as the average or less than the average. In any case, the estimates are incorporated in the numerator (formally being the free cash flows). However, if I attempt to fathom out how the beta is realised (and this has an influence on the denominator), it appears as though the same factors as outlined for the numerator also play a role. After all, I interpret the beta as follows. If the beta is greater than one, the value of the company fluctuates more than the fluctuations in the market index. If the beta is equal to one, the fluctuations are in line with the fluctuations in the market index. Finally, if the beta is less than one, the company has a value fluctuation that is more limited than the market index.

As far as I know, there is no literature covering the suspicion that the risk is possibly counted twice (incidentally, there is also no literature which rejects this). If the suspicion is correct, i.e. that it could be confirmed, I propose the following: incorporate the risk in the numerator (after all, we already use expected values there) and keep the denominator risk-free, so do not incorporate any risk increase via the beta in the denominator. After all, the effect of risk increases in the denominator is such that projects with higher expected cash flows in the long distant future are discriminated against in favour of projects with higher expected cash flows in the near future. In this way the calculation method could lead to longer term strategic thinking being penalised in favour of short-term alternatives and that must not be the case.'

It appears that there are a number of shortcomings in the use of the DCF method. Are there any alternatives to this?

Mr. Swagerman: 'It should be pointed out that the Discounted Cash Flow (DCF) method has contributed to the importance of future cash flows. The costs incurred in the past can be regarded as "sunk costs". For investment decisions only the future costs are important. Accounting return or past profits say nothing about the future profit capacity. At best, they give an indication of an historical pattern, which provides a forecast for the future development. Thinking in terms of future cash flows is one of the pillars of modern financing theory.

It has already been stated that there are objections to the use of the DCF method. There are currently some important developments taking place which partly accommodate the identified problems. These developments originate from option theory. This theory has found its first application in the hedging of financial risks. In addition, the option approach has been developed further and new applications within Corporate Finance have been found. In this connection, one possibility is to examine the relationship between shareholders and bondholders from a different point of view. The bondholder is equivalent to owing the firm assets, but giving a call option on these assets to the firm's stockholders (Bond value = asset value – value of call on assets). The

43

option approach is now being increasingly applied in other fields. Reference is than made to "real options".

With this "real options" approach a proper relationship can be made between Corporate Strategy and Corporate Finance. Many management decisions have an option-like character. In their decision-making, managers weigh up alternatives against one another and they usually do this in a more or less intuitive manner. In order to see these alternatives as an option possibility, a value can be given to them. In many decision-making cases it appears that there are embedded option aspects. These are the "real options". In the traditional DCF method, the flexibility employed by the management in its decision-making is underexposed. In contrast with the DCF method, the "real options" approach is based on the "contingent" character. The "real options" approach is, for example, already used for IT investments, value of learning effects, the possibility of "withdrawing" etc. Projects that would be rejected on the basis of DCF analysis still have a chance of being accepted by the "real option" approach.

I expect that the influence of the "real options" approach will be considerable in the future in the decision-making process. The management must master this form of thinking: it is all about the decision-making with respect to the value of the investment alternatives. It should be borne in mind that it is particularly uncertainty, which the management loathes in principle, that can create value.'

What can be said in general about the use of derivatives?
Mr. Swagerman: 'Although there is a major risk if they are used incompetently, the use of derivatives is generally regarded as one of the most important assets of financial management. Derivatives are used both to hedge positions and to realise extra profits. That is why their use has increased so much. In many cases, the supervisors are very worried about this. Time and again, the Bank of International Settlements (BIS) has tightened up the guidelines for the use of derivatives. It is impossible to establish whether this is adequate. Happily, the number of accidents resulting from the incompetent use of derivatives has decreased as a result of the increased knowledge and the further refinement of the essential business controls.

I would like to make a comment about the use of derivatives for the hedging of risks. In a perfect, efficient market the use of derivatives will not lead to additional profit because risk can only be shifted and not eliminated. In order to shift the risk, costs must be incurred for the financial instrument. Theoretically speaking, these costs are the same as the benefits to be obtained. In practice, it appears that the efficient market is to a great extent merely a theoretical concept and that derivatives can remove these market imperfections. Only the use of derivatives for those specific circumstances that counteract market imperfections can lead to value creation.

However, it is desirable to hedge transactions, despite the fact that there is an efficient market. The hedging, whether using derivatives or not, serves to ensure the continuity of the company and to avoid running – disproportional – risks. What I would also like to bring up with respect to the use of derivatives is the difference between risk hedging and risk control. This point of departure is still sometimes forgotten!

The option approach, whereby every management decision can be regarded as a "real option", i.e. the choice between "making a decision or not", is a very interesting development. It is all about indicating the value of alternatives. The more uncertain the circumstance, the higher the value to be derived from it. This new form of thinking in alternatives and the handling of risks will have an influence. With this it is possible to forge a relationship between corporate strategy and corporate finance'.

Does management have sufficient knowledge about the use of derivatives?
Prof. Bilderbeek: 'University courses in the financial field are currently covering the subject of derivatives quite adequately, so the younger managers with an economic or managerial background do have the knowledge. The modern financial manager is concerned with risk management to a great extent; this is quite different from how it was in the past.

Let me give you an example. If you look at reports in the press about local government banking activities, it seems that irresponsible risks are sometimes taken on account of the inadequate knowledge of management and board members. People should be aware of the fact that the unhedged writing of puts can actually lead to unlimited risk. Some fail to understand that the potential loss can be much greater than the costs of the financial instrument and the underlying security. Those in charge should be fully aware of these risks, but unfortunately this does not always seem to be the case.

I also see other fields in which the knowledge about derivatives is inadequate. Consider, for example, the issue of option rights given to the management. The Supervisory Board issues these rights and should make certain that they know what the consequences are. I think that the members of the Supervisory Boards of smallish companies do not always have insight into the technicalities of these issued rights. Slowly but surely it is sufficiently well known that use must not be made of inside knowledge when exercising management options. The company enters into commitments that it must comply with when the option rights are exercised.

In the coming years, these developments will substantially increase the demand for additional knowledge about the operation and use of derivatives from managers/board members/supervisors who do not have any specific financial training.'

What is the situation with regard to the incorporation of derivatives in the financial statements?

Mr. Swagerman: 'The incorporation of derivatives in the financial statements will exercise many minds in the coming years. The subject matter is extremely difficult so that there will be considerable demand for additional knowledge about valuation issues in the near future. FASB 133 "Accounting for Derivative Instruments and Hedging Activities" requires fair value accounting for all stand-alone derivatives; this particular statement is one of the most complex accounting standards ever issued. As a result of this, derivatives can no longer be regarded as an off-balance item. The derivatives must be shown on the balance sheet at their fair value and transactions must be shown in the profit and loss account. With this forthcoming change we also see an irreversible trend of the influence of the fair value principle in the reporting. This has consequences for our outlook on a number of prudential principles. Annual accounts are mainly based on the accounting concept of profit, so this principle will be partly abandoned in this new approach.'

Which developments are observed in the field of financial management?

Mr. Swagerman: 'The comment has already been made that the use of derivatives, including "real options", will increase in all kinds of fields. Another trend that I see is the further development of "experimental economics". "Game theory" has already been known for a long time. In this field, all kinds of interesting applications, such as the "prisoner's dilemma", have been under discussion. The application of "experimental economics" initially lay more in the field of micro-economics and political economy. Nowadays, on account of the increase in the number of auctions on Internet, there is a need for a statement about the behaviour of participants in a business environment. The more traditional economic theory provides few possibilities to make statements about the behaviour of the participants. An explanation of behaviour based on "behavioural economics" aspects has already been dealt with in the interview with Professor Benartzi in this book. Economic experiments in a laboratory environment can be used to predict behaviour in various circumstances.

Another important development is the influence of IT on the financial function. The extensive use of IT facilitates all kinds of developments which were previously impossible. The fields of financial management and IT will increasingly grow towards one another. Reference is therefore quite rightly made to Finance/IT. If we look at the use of the chipcard, for example, we can see that it creates entirely new possibilities for the user. The electronic wallet makes small payment transactions easier. We can, for instance, pay the parking meter with the chipcard and make other small payments. There are also other applications where the dominance of IT is asserting itself, one example of this being Internet banking. This application will result in major changes in the financial sector. Consumers are able to trade directly on the stock exchange via Internet. What will happen to the intermediary, the bank or the broker? It is likely that the current system is subject to changes.

A point that should not be underestimated in the use of IT for the financial function are the demands ensuing from internal and business controls. The design of the financial processes is being re-engineered by IT. The business controls will also have to be modified. The classical form of the segregation of duties will be reinforced by business controls that are incorporated as EDP controls. In this respect, there is certainly a role for the auditors here advising the company management about the correct use of their controls.

There are still a number of classical problems from the world of Corporate Finance that will also require attention in the future. First of all, the problem of the optimum capital structure must not go unmentioned. During the past few years, a lot of insight has been obtained about leverage and the relationship between shareholders' equity and debt. The option approach also plays a role when considering the methods of financing. It emerges from the Modigliani-Miller theorem that it makes no difference for the entrepreneur how the activities are financed. This may all be true but it still doesn't give us an answer to the question what the capital structure should look like for the organisation in question.'

How are the developments in the treasury function viewed?

Mr. Swagerman: 'Let me illustrate the development of the treasury function with the example of (municipal or provincial) government's banking activities. A lot has already been written about this subject. I would like to approach the discussion from a different angle. The task of every organisation is to efficiently manage scarce resources. For this reason, it is a good idea to lend temporary surpluses on the market and to borrow funds on the market to finance deficits. Waste would occur if the government did not perform effective liquidity management. This latter problem justifies government's treasury activities. The consequence is that policy will have to be formulated. In this connection there must be a treasury statute. This document, which must be approved by the policy supervisor (i.e. the local council or provincial authority), formulates points of departure, objectives, reporting method etc. In view of the fact that social resources are involved, meticulousness is a very important factor here. This means that those who approve the policy must know what the consequences of this approval are. The question is whether the supervisor is sufficiently able to form a picture of the problems resulting from modern financial constructions. Since the material is complicated, there may be a lack of knowledge, which could lead to an over-rash decision-making procedure. Obviously, Corporate Governance, as a subject of discussion for the business community, is also applicable in the case of government. Of course, the advantage for the government in this respect is that it should by definition already be familiar with the governance principles.

Treasury policy can also include the use of derivatives. It is, however, highly debatable whether (local) government should actually employ derivatives in its financial policy if there is insufficient knowledge available. The use of derivatives is relevant for the hedging of risk. Derivatives must certainly not be used for obtaining additional income. Financial institutions have considerable expertise in this field due to the fact that they are frequently confronted with derivatives. This knowledge is lacking among parties that are only occasionally concerned with "financial engineering". In this connection, it goes without saying that (local) government must not proceed with the writing of (unhedged) options, should avoid the OTC market as much as possible and always ensure that there is a closed position.

Up until now, the discussion has not paid enough attention to the relationship between the size and significance of the financial function and the treasury policy to be pursued. An organisation whose financial function is limited in size cannot achieve the necessary "economies-of-scope" and "economies of scale" to adequately support the treasury organisation. A difficult problem is indicating the point at which this function can be independently realised. If the decision to establish an independent treasury organisation is taken too lightly, an additional risk is faced. The supervisors will then have to ascertain whether the organisation in question is sufficiently qualified to independently perform the treasury function.

In my opinion, the entire discussion has not yet adequately dealt with the question why (municipal or provincial) government should maintain reserves so large that substantial sums have to be invested on the market. If there is a structural surplus, the reserves should be given back and the income volume of these government bodies should be reviewed. In general, the financial reserves can be at a lower level than in the business world since the risks faced are also lower. Although a favourable result can be realised by using financial instruments effectively, the agency costs must not be forgotten. These costs certainly weigh more heavily in the public sector than in the private sector and they can be much higher than the realisable return. Politicians and supervisors should also include this aspect of the agency costs in all their considerations.

Banking activities by local or central government can in general be regarded as the shift of treasury from a "cost centre" to a "profit centre". We do not see this as a favourable development, however. It would be better to migrate from a "cost centre" to a "service centre" concept. The treasury activities can be detached from the existing organisation. Similar treasury activities can be amalgamated. In this connection it is not about an organisational modification, such as the creation of an independent administrative body or privatisation measures, but about combining specific activities to obtain sufficient "economies-of-scope" and "economies-of-scale". At the moment, some housing corporations are successfully applying this possibility. Likewise, consideration could be given to the outsourcing of the treasury function to a financial institution. Partly on account of the influence of IT that leads to lower costs, organisations are increasingly confronted with this question. The government should take example from these developments, although the political will to do this must be present. Naturally, the institutional framework plays a role in the possible solution. Does the (municipal or provincial) supervisor want to place these activities at "arms length"? How are the developments that have already been initiated in this field evaluated?'

3. Hot topics in strategic finance

In conversation with Professor A.B. Dorsman
and Professor A. Thibeault

Risk management is in principle a very important activity in a company. Naturally, the question can be asked: how much risk can a company take and thus how much risk must be avoided or managed by a company. If you look at risk from the shareholders' point of view it can be assumed that particular excessive risks in a company can be avoided by diversifying, thus by also buying shares in companies where this risk is either less or the reverse. The question therefore is whether one regards the company as being purely shareholder-oriented or as stakeholder-oriented, i.e. the company as the place where the interests of a larger group of interested parties than just the shareholder converge. This important subject was discussed with two prominent Finance professors, Dorsman and Thibeault. In addition, the pre-eminent instrument for measuring risks at the moment, i.e. the Value at Risk, was also covered. What are the dangers of this and is it not wielded in a rather superficial manner?

The operation of the financial markets, partly with reference to the financial markets in the US, was also covered in some detail. The interview was concluded with the question whether Dorsman and Thibeault think that their current jobs will change fundamentally after the turn of the

Prof. A. Thibeault

Prof. A.B. Dorsman

century. Both finance professors firmly believe in the adequate and cleansing effect of the markets and that there is not a lot of polishing up to be done. Other contributions can evaluate whether the academic vision is also experienced the same way in practice.

André Thibeault completed his MBA at Université Laval in Quebec and at York University in Toronto and completed his PhD in Business Administration at the University of Western Ontario. Up until 1992 he was attached to Université Laval in various functions and in 1993 moved to Belgium where he was visiting Professor of Finance at FUCAM in Mons. In 1994, he joined Nyenrode University to start the Centre for Finance and to head the ING Chair of Financial Services and Risk Management. Since 1996, he has been Chairman of the Nyenrode Centre for Finance. He specialises in research in the field of banking and insurance and is (co-) author of several articles, including a number in the field of credit risk management.

André Dorsman is Professor of Finance at Nyenrode, senior researcher of Palladyne Asset Management and is also active at the Free University of Amsterdam. At Nyenrode, he is director of the Chartered Financial Analysis programme and also director of the postgraduate Chartered Principal Trading Specialist (CPTS) programme. In addition, he is chairman of both Royal NIVRA's Finance group and Financial Instruments group. He is an author of books about financial management and capital structure and capital market, and is also (co-) author of a number of articles in the field of corporate finance and investment analyses.

Is there sufficient risk management in companies or do they usually just react to developments and then start thinking about the problem?

Prof. Thibeault: 'I think they are initially taken by surprise. My feeling is that big companies react to what happens in the market and then try to put a risk management programme in place that makes sense from the point of view of the managers, but may not make sense from the point of view of the shareholders. Shareholders can always reduce risk by diversifying their own portfolio, but the situation is completely different for managers. In my opinion, the latter should use the financial market to replicate what an insurance company can do. Various risk management techniques based on the capital market, such as credit derivatives, are starting to make a big difference and make the job of the manager much safer, although they do not necessarily make companies more profitable. If you look at things from the shareholders' point of view you have to look at the potential bankruptcy costs and the type of risk you want to cover. Naturally, everyone looks at risk from a different point of view, but ultimately everyone involved wants to make sure that cash flows are sufficient and that bankruptcy is avoided.

There is of course a big difference in risk from one company to another. A very specialised company, for example, which has only one product is more at risk and faces a greater chance of bankruptcy than a company that is more diversified. A bancassurance company like ING has risk on the liability side because of its insurance operations as well as risk on the asset side because of its banking operations, but this form of risk management requires the creation of a conglomerate.

From a risk management point of view it does make sense to merge insurance, investment banking and commercial banking operations.

If I look at the international financial sector, which is the sector I know best, I would say that it has started moving towards the Anglo-Saxon system during the past ten to fifteen years. This means that profitability and the shareholders' point of view is more and more important. If the shareholders' point of view is becoming so important then I would argue that you shouldn't hedge all the risk because otherwise you won't make any money.'

If the shareholder value is of vital importance you should minimise risk management because you have diversification, but if you act in the interest of all stakeholders you need more sophisticated risk management. What is your opinion about this?

Prof. Dorsman: 'You should look at developments over time. Look at the position of labour, for example. There is currently a shortage on the labour market, quite a different situation to twenty years ago. Workers can now accept more risk than they did in the past because they can more easily change their jobs. In my opinion, there is actually no difference between the position of labour and the position of capital where the management of risk is concerned. All stakeholders, whether they are managers, employees, suppliers or shareholders are all willing to accept a certain level of risk management. It seems to me that the level of risk management in companies can be lower than the level that treasury departments consider necessary. Perhaps I should also make one comment about the suppliers of a company. Companies are now returning to their core business, one reason being that it is no longer necessary to secure their supply. Ten or twenty years ago you had to invest in your suppliers in order to guarantee supplies, but that is no longer essential. There is no risk where supply is concerned because there are enough products on the market and I believe that this is the main reason for concentrating on the core business.'

Is there a difference in the perception of a major shareholder and the holder of just a few shares in a company?

Prof. Thibeault: 'Probably not, because the Anglo-Saxon way of looking at value creation from the shareholder's point of view is based on the assumption that nobody holds a major part of the company and that everybody who holds a share in the company is well diversified. If the shareholder is not very well diversified then the assumption on which we base value creation for the maximisation of the share price does not hold. On the other hand, if you have a major shareholder with a lot of concentration in one company, then risk management begins to be very important.'

Prof. Dorsman: 'There is certainly a difference in the response of the different shareholders to changes in company policy. The small shareholder tends to do nothing, while the large shareholders make a calculated choice. This is something I witnessed recently when Rodamco, a real estate investment company, was split into four separate companies, each with a different geographical focus. The large shareholders thought about investing in real estate in North America or Asia and even considered other possibilities, while the small shareholders didn't make any choice at all, they just waited to see what would happen. The larger shareholders have an opinion about a company's investments and they express that opinion, but what can a small shareholder say? And if they do not say anything, how can their wishes be taken into account?'

Prof. Thibeault: 'If small shareholders are concerned about avoiding risk you would assume that they would diversify. It would therefore seem wise for them to buy mutual funds instead of individual shares.'

What is your opinion about the level of transparency of the market in North America compared to that in Europe?

Prof. Dorsman: 'I think there's a very big difference in transparency and that is perhaps the reason why some groups in Europe have a lot more influence on the boards of companies than they do in the US, for instance. The information required by the SEC, the US regulator, is much more detailed than that required by the Dutch regulator. For example, you need to spend three days filling in the SEC's forms, while it only takes about half a day to complete the Dutch forms, so there is a lot of difference between them. That's also the problem when you are talking about insider trading. In the US, an insider, whether a large shareholder, the management, or just someone buying or selling stock, has to inform the Securities and Exchange Commission.'

Prof. Thibeault: 'The difference is also apparent if you look at the examination requirements to obtain the Chartered Financial Analyst title. Ethics is a major element, not in terms of coverage, but it is well known that if you don't pass the ethics part of the CFA 1 examination, for example, you will not pass the examination at all. Transparency is therefore very important in North America and I think it is also evolving here. The European Centre for Ethics at Nyenrode is doing a lot of work in the field and many financial institutions are asking them to do special work for them.'

Do you think that the difference between the financial markets and the real markets is too large? What do you think about keeping people like George Sores, the influential financier, under control by means of more government regulation of the markets?

Prof. Thibeault: 'We have to be careful about this because we all know that Mr. Greenspan said about a year ago that the market was getting out of control and then came back a few months later and said that it was possible to maintain such a growth rate because of improvements in technology and so on. The market is based on subjective assessment, and that has always been the case. People know that prices are based on expectations. I certainly do not think you should try to tax financial flows, I don't think it is feasible in practice and I believe that improved supervision and greater transparency would be much better. If you have more transparency and you know what people are doing then it is possible to maintain a market which is much more stable. That is what the Bank of International Settlements (BIS) is trying to do in the field of banking. Proper regulation will ensure that risk is taken into account and that there is enough transparency. Otherwise the danger is that a major bankruptcy might have a domino effect and produce economic outcomes that are unacceptable on the social level. Instead of talking about taxes, it is much better to have regulations to guarantee transparency and then people on the market will react accordingly.'

Prof. Dorsman: 'I think that the financial markets react to what people do on the real market. On this point I could cite the example of the City of Amsterdam that wants to restrict car access to the city centre. In response, organisations like the Amsterdam Zoo ask how people can visit it and threaten to submit a claim if such a step is taken. In the real economy, political parties and the government want to impose various policies and raise taxes, but the financial markets react and both governments and companies have to listen to them. So there is interaction between the financial market and the real market and I think this is good.'

Prof. Thibeault: 'In addition, I don't think that assessment on the real market is properly performed. Take inflation, for example. The inflation index in the Netherlands is generally said to be very, very low; but is this the case? Not really. If you look at the increase in the price of housing on a yearly basis you see quite the opposite. A lot of people in the financial sector are very concerned about the increase in the value of the stock exchange because they make a comparison with what is perceived as a low rate of inflation, but we know that real inflation is quite high. Looking at developments from this point of view, the market is not overreacting and is not only based on expectation and speculation.'

Returning to the subject of risk management, is Value at Risk (VAR) a useful scientific instrument?

Prof. Thibeault: 'It depends how you use it and for which instrument; the technique is fine as long as you apply it on the right underlying instrument. Most of the time it is based on historical data and does not include all the information. The VAR estimate may not identify a looming bankruptcy because of the information that is outside the range; people should not put too much faith in the tool. We have to remember that it is not the only tool for managing risks. There are times when I would prefer to use a technique that is not based on normal distribution. A few months ago, for example, the BIS refused to allow the bank to use its own internal system for credit risks, precisely because the distribution was not normal. Another problem in this respect is the correlation coefficient. If this coefficient is not stable you will compute a VAR that may make sense to you but is totally inaccurate.'

Prof. Dorsman: 'I believe there are two questions here. The first question is whether there is a better system than VAR. If you don't have a better system what choice do you have? The VAR tool provides a very clear-cut answer: based on this level of risk acceptance this is what you have to do. This is very clear, and people like clear solutions; they are not so interested in the ideas behind the conclusion. The second question is when you should use the VAR tool. I believe that if the situation is normal you can use it, but I don't think it is of any help in an abnormal situation.'

56

What is your evaluation of the euro, now that it has been in use for a year?

Prof. Thibeault: 'I am not a macro-economist so I can only give you a very general assessment. Where financial institutions are concerned, I do not think that the relative value of the euro compared to the US dollar is important. What is important for these institutions now that they are dealing in a single currency is how they position themselves on the European continent. You are now starting to see some major changes in strategy that partly relate to the introduction of the euro. For example, ING Bank was previously focused on emerging markets, but about two years ago the chairman of the Board stated that ING wanted to be a European bank. One of the reasons for the change in strategy relates to cash management and the introduction of the euro. As a result of the concentration that is taking place, Europe will perhaps only have four or five major players on the market so the focus of institutions must change.'

Prof. Dorsman: 'European unification has led to a major shift from small caps to large stocks. A reason for this is that US investment companies wanting to invest in Europe only look at the large companies. If you look at the development of the stock exchanges during the past half-year you see that the large stocks are going up and the small caps are going down. This is one of the results of the introduction of the euro. On top of this, the introduction of the euro has also had an effect on securitisation, the process of converting future cash flows into debt securities.'

In ten years time, will the Professor of Finance be more a Professor of IT or more a Professor of Strategy?

Prof. Thibeault: 'It's possible and this is borne out by the evolution of the finance function in universities, for example. When I started my study in finance, we were concerned with break-even analysis and with accounting information. Then we moved to the capital asset pricing model with diversification and this meant that we had to learn a little bit about statistics. Now we are moving into the field of risk management and are at the stage of determining how mathematics fits together with finance. Quite clearly, financial analysis is becoming more complex from a mathematical point of view and certainly involves a lot more information technology. Professors of Finance need to be very strong conceptually in order to avoid being fooled by statistics and mathematical analyses; the IT tools may be very sophisticated but they do not necessarily provide the right answers.

The link between finance and strategy depends upon how old you are. When you start your career as a young finance professor you are more concerned with the technical aspects, with a more quantitative approach. When you get older you start to feel that there is a strategic issue and I have seen many of my colleagues move from hi-tech finance to a more strategic point of view as they got older. This raises the question whether they are unable to adapt to the new requirements of the profession or whether they are getting smarter.'

Prof. Dorsman: 'Information technology is an essential tool for providing data, for analysing data and for performing statistical analyses. The job of the Professor of Finance is to provide a strategic overview of all this information and to weigh it up against a wider knowledge of the political system and other environmental factors. That is what Strategic Finance is all about.'

4. Theory and practice: inseparable pair?

In conversation with Professor L. Traas

As Austrian poet and philosopher Ernst Freiherr von Feuchtersleben (1806-1849) once said, 'Die Theorie ist nicht die Wurzel, sondern die Blüte der Praxis'. Theory is the flower rather than the root; it is the result rather than the origin. Put differently: the relationship between theory and practice is like body and soul. Scientist and practician Professor Lou Traas (1934) is a good judge of this matter. He is renowned as a Professor of Management Accounting and External Reporting at the Free University of Amsterdam and fulfils many prominent positions. To name a few: he is a supervisory director for several companies, he is a member of the Enterprise Section of the Court of Appeal and he plays a leading role in several prominent visitation committees.

Prof. L. Traas

We all know there are plenty of smart theories, but the question is: can they be applied in practice? And: does the real world actually need them? Think of all the extensive and in-depth discussions that followed various reports on, for example, corporate governance, accounting principles, efficiency and the self-regulatory nature of financial markets? Not to mention shareholder value and value based management.

Do these theories provide added value for companies and society as a whole?

Prof. Traas: 'Of course they do, although I admit that theory and practice often contradict each other. The problem is, on the one hand, that theories don't always take into account that the real world is a volatile place, and on the other hand, that theories are not always put into practice as they were meant to. Just think of the difference between theory and practice when taking a driving test. In theory, everything should go according to the rules. In reality, however, not everyone follows those rules and the theory cannot always be put into practice.

When I was working with Philips, from 1960 to 1970, eventually heading the Business Economics Department, the distance between the financial/accounting function and the executive management was much larger than it is today. The main focus at the time was on reporting after the fact. Profit – particularly Philips' notion of profit – was key. Decision calculations and business economic direction before the fact were novel concepts. In 1967, I wrote my thesis "A company's investment and funding plan" while I was a man in the business. I went into great detail on the theories written by Modigliani, Miller and other finance gurus. This proved to be a sound basis for my scientific activities and for practical teaching programmes in the late eighties, when the real world was finally ready for new trends emerging from financing theories.

It is a fact that I am in great favour of upgrading shareholder value. In my opinion, Value Based Management (VBM) is shareholder value put into practice. What I mean is that a well set-up VBM system can optimise shareholder value, provided it is translated properly at division and business unit levels, i.e. the business units within the company. Essentially, VBM should be formulated by way of targets and there should be a system in place to check that management is aware of these targets and that they are achieved. Such targets are often formulated in terms of Economic Value Added (EVA). Although targets can also be defined slightly differently, many companies opt for the EVA approach.

In order to define the EVA formula adequately and perform VBM properly, one should apply a cost of capital that reflects the return on investment demanded by the shareholders. The return on investment can be deduced from the share price level on the stock market and incorporated in the EVA formula. In addition, the correct asset basis (investment basis) has to be incorporated. In other words, important intangible assets such as goodwill, brands and customised software should be accounted for. If this is done accurately, a positive EVA clearly implies that the company or business unit in question is indeed creating shareholder value.

A second aspect is that value based management should not only be translated into accurate EVA concepts; it is also essential that the value drivers within the company and its business units be identified.

The problem is that although many companies use a concept that roughly resembles EVA, they are not accurate when it comes to the exact definition of the return on investment, or even of the investment base. Thus, they may produce a reasonably useful performance indicator with which they can compare the (terms of reference of the) budget with the actual results, but they miss the link with shareholder value that can be found if the EVA is defined properly. In other words, if you fail to define the basic elements accurately, a positive EVA does not necessarily imply that the company has realised shareholder value and visa versa. At the end of the day, that's what counts most of all. If you can only see whether your company has done better that budgeted, you might as well forget about the EVA. EVA is a sophisticated tool; if it is used inaccurately, it doesn't provide added value.'

You have said that Philips is a good example of properly implemented Value Based Management. Could you explain this?

Prof. Traas: 'Philips' performance is quite good. Both the definition of the accounting elements within EVA and the translation into value drivers for the management have to be carried out accurately in practice. In a number of ways, Philips has succeeded in doing so. The company puts a lot of effort (by means of large scale training courses and information meetings) into defining, on behalf of its management, the concept of value from the shareholders' perspective and to keep this issue in focus during regular meetings. I do have to remark, however, that Philips' accounting technique is not perfect. After all, Philips applies very few corrections in calculating the investment base. For an international company like Philips, I would have preferred to also adjust the required return on investment to the interest rates of those countries in which the company is active and to the risk levels of the various business units. So, although Philips is a good example of VBM, it is not yet perfect.

Another example I'd like to mention is Heijmans, a relatively small contractor which has applied the VBM line throughout its annual report for 1998 and thus informs outsiders of how it is doing in terms of value creation.

I think this is a good way of presenting oneself. There are countless companies which proudly announce at press conferences or during meetings that they are applying EVA aimed at improving or maintaining investor relations, but which fail to explicate their criteria and return requirements and the way in which they assess and treat their new investments. This is why I commend Heijmans, who has set forth all these matters in its annual report. In the USA, Quaker Oats was always a pioneer in this respect, but now the Dutch company Heijmans has taken it one step further.'

Critics of EVA claim the concept leads to short-term thinking. They say that the DCF method can also be applied to decisions and that it provides a better indicator than EVA.

Prof. Traas: 'I have indeed heard these comments. However, the critics seem to forget that the result produced by EVA is basically the same as that of DCF, provided it is applied accurately. DCF produces a percentage, but if you apply net present value, it produces an absolute figure. EVA also produces an absolute figure, albeit on an annual basis. If you calculate the present value of the expected EVAs for a project or a business unit, you get the present value of that project or business unit. In my 1967 thesis, I already argued that the calculation of an EVA pattern for a project could serve as a sound investment selection method. At the time, I referred to it as the "profit profile" of a project. This provides more insight than the DCF rate or the absolute amount of the net present value. However, a "profit profile" is basically the same as the pattern of the future EVAs. In that respect, my thesis was an "EVA avant la lettre". Effectively, I don't believe there is any difference between EVA and DCF, provided the EVAs are calculated for the same period.

Another point of discussion is the correlation between EVA and the development of the share price. Of course one can always perform statistical tests to try to establish correlations. Sometimes, researchers start searching for correlations without having given it much consideration. I believe these types of studies are pointless. One knows in advance that the outcome will be a poor correlation. The correlation between EVA and share prices is a case in point. After all, EVA reflects how much shareholder value a company's sales in a given financial year have generated. However, we must bear in mind that share prices do not only react to the outcome of a single financial year, but rather to expectations for a series of years in future.

Being an internal performance indicator, EVA can never correspond perfectly with share prices. If for example a company invents a wonderful product that is very promising, this will not be reflected in the EVA of the current period, but it will definitely affect the share price. There could be a parallel between the expected EVAs for future years on the one hand and the development of the share price on the other. However, the day-to-day management of a company has little or no use for such a forecast. Therefore, the two have to be separated. One the one hand there is the future oriented information to which the share price reacts. On the other, there is EVA as a performance indicator per period which best inspires the management to take those actions that maximise the company's value in the long term.'

Do you believe that strategic/financial decisions like mergers and acquisitions are often the result of subjective, impulsive decisions by the Chief Executive Officer? Something in the sense of: if the competition does it, I should be doing it as well.

Prof. Traas: 'No, I don't think so. Perhaps these types of decisions, at strategic level, used to be made in this fashion but this is certainly no longer the case. In the Netherlands, in particular, such decisions are not made lightly. Of course, when unexpected changes take place, companies have to react quickly. You might say that ABN-AMRO had been sleeping for ten years, causing it to miss out on its bid for the Belgian Generale Bank, but why should it have taken action when the entire business was hibernating? If Walmart were to become active in Europe, I could imagine that certain competitors would start feeling uncomfortable. This could give them the impulse to become active as well, lest they lag behind. But a reaction upon an unexpected event is not necessarily impulsive. In the past, there have been many panic acquisitions. I believe many companies are now very prudent when it comes to mergers and acquisitions. Of course, they have learned from their mistakes. For example, the merger between Bols, originally a liquor company, and Wessanen, a food company, or the merger between KNP, a paper company and Bührmann Tetterode, a wholesaler in office furniture and graphic equipment. These mergers didn't survive long and have already been undone.

Corporate management realise that there have to be obvious advantages to a merger. An unsuccessful merger is not only an embarrassment to undo, it also causes the shareholders to lose their faith in the Board of Management and Supervisory Board concerned.'

Nonetheless, one cannot deny that some companies benefit from ad-hoc opportunities rather than follow a strategic plan.

Prof. Traas: 'I'm not sure that's true. I do however see that large and medium-sized companies nowadays take careful consideration of their strategy, which they continuously monitor in view of changes in markets, technologies and competition. But always asking oneself whether one is following the right path does not mean that the strategic concept is set aside. At management level, there has to be a clear strategy; if not, operational management will not be motivated and the company will sway and go adrift. The ship needs to follow a certain course but if bad weather comes up, the ship has to be able to deviate from that course. And if interesting opportunities arise, it would be unwise to let them go by.

I still believe that mergers and acquisitions are rarely entered into on the spur of the moment. Indeed, they are matters of patience. There are many examples of mergers and acquisitions that were preceded by a long period of courting. And even then, many acquisitions are abandoned at the last moment. Not for nothing, most businesses keep in close contact with competitors and potential partners, enabling them to collect valuable information and explore their options.'

What is your opinion on the business world's reaction to the report on corporate governance issued by the Peters Committee?

Prof. Traas: 'The Peters Committee deserves a compliment for its work. Nonetheless, I think the business world is losing interest in this subject. I don't believe in the spontaneous further development of corporate governance now that "Peters" has given the signal to start, so to speak.

As regards corporate governance, we can distinguish three elements. Firstly, shareholder control, particularly in the form of anti-takeover measures and secondly, corporate control. The Committee has argued that companies should disclose more with regard to their management control system. Thirdly, transparency of the management policy itself.

Public opinion has mainly focused on shareholder control and anti-takeover measures. As a result, some things have changed in this respect and there is also a bill currently in preparation. At the end of the day, what is likely to evolve is that majority shareholders will be granted the right to bid for the remainder of a company's shares. The Enterprise Section of the Court of Appeal, together with specific experts, will then have to assess whether the bid is supported by a policy concept that justifies the take-over action. This will probably solve the control issue.

What does still call for further attention is the issue of disclosure regarding the manner in which companies are managed. Particularly significant – and this is where the relevance of external reporting comes in – is the transparency of the company's management policy. I am referring to the disclosure of strategy, risk profile, (future) trends in markets and technologies, human resource policy, environmental policy etc. I must say I am a lot less optimistic in this regard. If the government or some other central body fails to take the lead from the Peters

Committee, its recommendations will become diluted and we will be left with very little.

Consequently, new legislation aimed at granting shareholders more control will have little effect. After all, control can only be exercised with adequate information and if there is insufficient disclosure, the information won't be adequate. If information is lacking, shareholders simply will not have much to discuss with the management. Incidentally, I don't believe policy and control issues are likely to be discussed at shareholders' meetings. Those who have ever attended a shareholders' meeting know that in-depth and fruitful discussions with the management do not tend to take place there. No, the essence is transparency vis-à-vis the outside world, so as to allow reactions from for example the press, analysts and within the framework of investor relations.

In the Netherlands, we have a very poor system of regulations regarding external reporting. We have the Corporations Act, that is over 30 years old, amended about twenty years ago to comply with European directives. And then there's the Council for Annual Reporting, which gives recommendations and sometimes issues statements, although companies are not obliged to comply with these.

The Council for Annual Reporting usually follows IASC directives, albeit with some delay, but these directives are merely recommendations. The Dutch membership of the IASC means no more than that the auditor is bound to do his utmost to apply the rules within companies. From a corporate law perspective, it is said that the Netherlands is a haven of refuge where reporting requirements are concerned.

And then of course, there's the directors' report: that part of the annual report which comes on top of the pure financial statements. In the Netherlands, we don't have regulations similar to the SEC requirements in the US for the section on Management Discussion & Analysis (MD&A). This is remarkable, given that the director's report – according to many – is the most important part of the annual report. In the US, the SEC is not even satisfied with the current situation, while their audit requirements are much stricter than ours. In addition to the already extensive US regulations, the SEC is now promoting audit committees as important players in achieving a full-scale directors' report and a true and fair annual report. The SEC sees such audit committees as the ultimate guardians of corporate governance.

In general, we do not have audit committees in the Netherlands. We do have supervisory directors, but it must be said that this body's opinion usually supports that of the company's management. I think there is little hope for the two most important aspects of corporate governance: neither the management control structure nor the policy will be made transparent in sufficient detail until the regulations are drastically tightened and a body is appointed to act as "ultimate guardian".'

Are you saying that both corporate governance and external reporting lack any regulation in the Netherlands?

Prof. Traas: 'Even compared to non-Anglo Saxon countries, the Netherlands do not score well. Germany just recently issued an extensive directive on management reporting, which is more stringent than the British directive, although not as strict as the US rules.

The SEC has stated one basic rule for the MD&A: the shareholder is entitled to extrapolate. I see this as a fundamental rule. It means that the shareholder is entitled to assume that the company management believes the company's sales, cost and profit, as reflected by their annual report, will follow the same trend in the future, unless the management has explicitly stated otherwise. I acknowledge that the management cannot be expected to know everything, but they should not hold back information that is essential to the formulation of future expectations. If they seek a turning point or a change in policy, this should be disclosed. This is quite a bit more than we are accustomed to here in the Netherlands. In many Dutch companies, the directors' report is downright incomplete when it comes to information which is relevant for the future. As far as I'm concerned, the shareholder should be granted the right to extrapolate in the Netherlands as well. This is in line with the concept of corporate governance. After all, the way in which a company is managed is of concern to all those involved; even society as a whole, which leaves a part of the societal production process to each company and should therefore be entitled to knowing how the company is doing. Companies that do not comply should be publicly denounced.

Fortunately, there are several Dutch companies that do pay a lot of attention to their annual report. Either they consider it important to keep up a reputation of being a modern company or their competitors in the Anglo Saxon world present elaborate annual reports (in compliance with local requirements) and they prefer not to lag too far behind. Nevertheless, this is a minority, which, when it comes to the crunch and appears that certain information may have a negative effect, also tend to hide themselves behind the lack of regulations in the Netherlands.'

Do option schemes for managers give them a good reason to disclose less and bend information somewhat? Perhaps even manipulate information in order to receive a better reward?

Prof. Traas: 'The idea behind option schemes is to link reward to result. I don't think that is a bad principle. However, a short-term focus has to be avoided in option schemes. Many companies do this by granting options which are executable only after two or three years and within a certain period of time. This helps prevent short-term policy making.

By the way, option schemes in the Netherlands may soon come almost to an end, since the Minister of Finance has made them unattractive tax-wise. Besides, there is always the chance that options do not yield much and that the share price doesn't exceed the execution price.

Perhaps worth mentioning is the option scheme promoted by US consultants Stern & Stewart. We were speaking about EVA earlier. Consulting firm Stern & Stewart, virtually the founders of EVA, has integrated this system with the option scheme; not a bad idea if you ask me. Stewart does not give options and bonuses on the basis of the difference between the current and future share price. Instead, profit growth incorporated in the share price is taken as the basis. This profit growth is what they try to deduce. Then, bonus schemes are agreed which grant the manager a bonus if he achieves a higher profit growth than that which is incorporated in the share price. Moreover, a bonus bank is created, in which the money is held in escrow until it is paid out, with some delay. This is an interesting approach.

I am not at all against option schemes. However, I would like to see schemes that are safeguarded from abuse. This implies that options should be held for a considerable period of time, say two or three years. To avoid insider trading, one could stipulate that options can only be executed after the CEO or the Supervisory Directors have been notified. Thus, if there were sensitive issues within the company, they would provide a barrier.'

Is there a clear relationship between corporate governance and the value of a company? In other words, would the value increase if it were to be announced that the Anglo Saxon system of corporate governance were to be adopted?

Prof. Traas: 'I cannot imagine that the annulment of anti-takeover measures as a result of corporate governance would affect the value of the company. In the early nineties, it was claimed that the value of Dutch shares was low due to the heavy burden of anti-takeover measures. Meanwhile, not much has changed in the field of anti-takeover measures and yet some are now claiming that Dutch shares are overvalued. In short, the whole thing is imagined.

On the one hand, not a single anti-takeover measure is completely airtight. A takeover bid can only be delayed, not avoided entirely. The downward effect on the value of the company is therefore limited. On the other hand, I do believe that if corporate governance were to result in more disclosure and more certainty about the company's activities, the cost of capital would decrease as the shareholders would have more faith in what was happening to their investment. So, if the reporting were to provide more in-depth and strategic information, the risk would basically be lower. In that case, the value of the company would indeed go up.'

Isn't the gap between financial and real markets too big? Are things under control or are we heading for an economic crisis since no one has any grip on the financial markets?

Prof. Traas: 'Globalisation and the expansion of the information society will continue. We are living in a borderless society. That is a fact that nobody can turn back. The world is getting smaller and easier to control. Of course, it is important that reliable information is available, for example about crises. One of the causes of the Asia crisis was that there was insufficient information about the scope of the dollar loans and foreign currency obligations entered into by companies and governments.

It might be wise to somewhat restrict the speculative capital movements in world trade. Now, billion dollar transactions can cause markets to implode. In such cases, it should be possible to take far-reaching measures to limit the consequences. This becomes a yo-yo effect, which I believe can be limited by creating boundaries for speculative capital movements. This calls for regulations.'

Can these matters be solved at a national level?

Prof. Traas: 'No, absolutely not; not with the imminent arrival of the euro. It has to be tackled for each currency region.'

Many large multinational companies were caught off-guard by the Asia crisis. Are we, in the Netherlands, adequately prepared for such developments?

Prof. Traas: 'Of course there is a lot of room for improvement, particularly in respect of treasury policy. Risk management in the financial field should be tackled by a consistent treasury policy. It is vital that this policy be clearly formulated within the company, that the targets be communicated and that the requirements for currencies, exposure, interest management and short and long-term funding be unambiguous. There should be clear objectives and limits with respect to the ratio between short-term and long-term funding. The ratio between debt and equity should be well motivated. I believe there should be clear policy lines within the company on the use of derivatives.

If the policy lines were to become too complicated, the company should have independent consultants study the entire procedure. I do think there is a lack of adequate risk management within companies. In many cases, a director or supervisory director signs something he hasn't read or understood properly. The management cannot be expected to know everything but should realise they are responsible and consequently make sure – for example on the basis of an audit by external experts – that their "system" for "risk management" is adequate.'

What should a good financial expert know before entering the new millennium?

Prof. Traas: 'Some fear that finance has become too computerised, mathematical and statistical. I believe that as far as the main perspective of the financial function is concerned, there won't be much change. I have always remembered a passage by Gordon Donaldson, Professor of Finance at the Harvard Business School. In 1970, he quoted, in his book "Strategy for Financial Mobility", the annual report of Philips in order to illustrate the core of the financial function. In that annual report, there was a paragraph devoted to financial executive Willem de Jonge, who was leaving the company at the time. The Board thanked De Jonge for his efforts: he had always ensured that there was enough money available, that transactions – no matter how large – could be funded and that he never had to call things to a halt due to a lack of funds. Donaldson's conclusion in this respect: "He ensured that the profitability of the company was such that there was always access to the financial markets." In my opinion, that is still the quintessence of the financial function: to keep a sharp eye on the business so that there is always access to the financial markets and the channels to those markets are used optimally.

Should a finance manager become an IT expert? No, I don't think so. As long as he has a good command of his profession and ensures that the company is profitable. In that respect he holds a key position, albeit a less prominent one. You could say his position is adjacent to or just behind the general management, the head of the business unit or the chairman of the board. He has to keep close tabs of the business and take immediate action when things go wrong; i.e. when there is less profit. I believe there are too many financial experts who are overly concerned about the financial markets and treasury and who know so little about the business of their own company that they find it difficult to assess when and how they should take action in the internal and operational affairs of that business. The financial experts should above all be capable of constructive thinking as to the strategic path of the company. That is what we should try to teach them during their schooling.'

5. Portfolio theory is still the starting point for many decisions

In conversation with Professor H. Markowitz

As the Latin poet Ovid was already aware, 'mankind is sure of nothing'. And indeed, as long as man has existed, he has been in search of explanations for certain phenomena. He does this not only to satisfy his curiosity, but also to use his knowledge to understand those events that remain unexplained, arbitrary, unpredictable and therefore frightening. These events serve not only to confuse him, but they may also threaten his very existence. And so man turns to research to track down the laws to which many events are subjected. A rich harvest is awaiting anyone who is able to make accurate predictions about the weather or disasters; he can follow the right course, and seek safety in good time. In short, anyone with knowledge and experience readily imagines himself to be the master of a situation. Whoever understands the market – whether it be the corn market, the currency market or the stock market – sees the opportunities open up before him. But, what are the risks involved, and how can you measure them? How do they influence the return? Where is the fine line between inspired guesswork and well-founded decisions? How should you go about putting together the best possible share portfolio? And... is it actually possible?

Prof. H. Markowitz

It is to these questions that Prof. Harry Markowitz (1927) set out to find an answer. His fifteen-page article 'Portfolio Selection' was published in 1952 in The Journal of Finance. From that moment on, Markowitz became a legend – an institution in his own right. So much so that he was awarded the Nobel Prize for economics in 1990, an honour that he shared with two other colleagues.

Professor Markowitz' career has focused rather more on operations research than on finance.

He himself considers the portfolio theory to be applied operations research in the fields of finance, mathematics and informatics.

After graduating he went to work for the RAND Corporation in Santa Monica, an organisation he describes as 'a kind of air force think-tank'. Here he developed both the simulation techniques for the analysis of air force logistics, and the techniques for optimising those logistics. At RAND he also developed a computer language suited to putting together simulations, enabling the computer to function as if it were a factory or a transportation system. Together with a colleague he started up a software company to sell this language and to develop it further. However, after about five years they had differences of opinion, and Markowitz left the company. He then worked as a professor for one year, but at the time it did not particularly interest him. He also managed his own investment funds for a couple of years.

He then went to work at the IBM research centre in New York, where he returned to information science. So, throughout his entire career he has been involved with many different things – with optimisation techniques, information science, financial analysis and portfolio theory. The common denominator in all these things was the application of mathematical and computer techniques to practical problems.

After about ten years with IBM Research he received a call from the president of the Baruch College, a faculty at the University of New York City. He was asked whether he would be interested in holding a chair that had become vacant at the university, and that's where he stayed until he retired in 1993. He then returned to California to start up a consultancy which he is still running.

It is difficult to overestimate the influence Markowitz' ideas have had. Though it did take some ten years before his theories could be applied. The reason being that the calculations necessary to apply his model were very complex for that time. In 1963, W.F. Sharpe managed to simplify the Markowitz model. In his *'A simplified model for portfolio analysis'*, published in Management Science, he introduced his Single Index Model that could be used to select shares for a portfolio.

Nevertheless Markowitz was the first person to demonstrate that the risk/expected return ratio could be optimised by selecting efficient portfolios. Given a particular level of risk it is possible to determine for every portfolio the fractions of the shares that together will give the highest yield.

Markowitz' theory is based on the premise that financial assets can be assessed by weighing up the yield and the risk. Portfolio theory makes it possible to quantify these considerations. What we are looking at is the relationship between the financial benefits and the risks. This is referred to in statistics as the covariance. It is also possible that the risk of the portfolio taken as a whole is less than the sum of the separate risks of the individual shares that go to make up the portfolio. If a particular share reacts negatively to external changes, a different share may increase in value: when oil prices decrease, it has both a negative effect on the shares in an oil company and a positive effect on shares in an airline One compensates the other, thereby diminishing the total risk. According to Markowitz, what we need to do is to find a mix achieving a balance with the lowest risks for a given return.

Markowitz' theory has had considerable influence on other theories and concepts. Among these is the 'value at risk concept', which has had a following among financial institutions for some time and which is also finding increasing application among industrial enterprises. The essence of this concept is also that risks can be quantified on the basis of data providing an insight into the extent of fluctuation of the parameters under investigation. But Markowitz is not only a statistical man, he also has a clear view of developments over the past few years in the finance area and is devoting himself to coming up with a better strategy.

Is it true that since the models of Markowitz, Sharpe, Black & Scholes, Jensen, Solnik, Ross, Modigliani & Miller and Fama, nothing new has really happened in the finance area?

Prof. Markowitz: 'I wouldn't put it quite like that. What is true is that portfolio theory is still relied on quite heavily. I wanted an answer to the question of how an investor could deploy his resources in the best way possible with the minimum of risk for a given return. This was the subject of my dissertation and everything I had to say on the matter can be found in my book that was published in 1959. Bill Sharpe continued along the same lines and wondered, among other things, what the market would look like if everyone complied with my theory on the efficient allocation of funds. He went on to develop the Capital Asset Pricing Model (CAPM), which has numerous applications. One application was the original work by Black & Scholes about the option values of resources. Their theory was actually an application of the Capital Asset Pricing Model with a few additional assumptions. Michael Jensen had a different application. He asked: "How should we measure the performance of the money managers?" When I was working on my dissertation, that performance was measured by taking a five to ten year period and looking at the returns of one particular money manager. No attention was given to any possible volatility. Jensen advanced the thesis that we should judge the money managers not on the basis of average return alone, but also on the basis of the fluctuations in the return, as with portfolio theory. His conclusion was that, on average, money managers didn't perform any better. On the basis of the research Wells Fargo Bank went on to create the "index funds".

Another example is "Riskmetrics", which is also an application stemming from portfolio theory, that is to say from a formula for the variability in a portfolio. This includes the covariance between individual securities. Riskmetrics gives estimates for the world stock markets. Although many developments are based on the portfolio theory, I wouldn't particularly like to claim that nothing new is being developed. Though I dare endorse the assertion that anyone who is familiar with the theories of Modigliani, Black & Scholes, Jensen, Sharpe and my own, would be able to understand some 99% of current developments. Once you are familiar with the basic principles of portfolio theory, the CAPM and "option pricing theory", you should be in a position to come up with much of the rest yourself.'

Nowadays many companies set great store by shareholders' value. Is this really the most important aim of a business?

Prof. Markowitz: 'I am absolutely convinced by Adam Smith's thesis that it is for the benefit of all when everyone attempts to maximise their own income and own utility in line with the rules and without deceiving anyone. There are two theories on this subject, one by Adam Smith and the other by Karl Marx. There are places in the world where the state owns the resources and where people are expected to serve the common interest. But since the grain that belongs to everyone belongs to no one, it doesn't take long before it's lying rotting in the fields.

The alternative is that people attempt to maximise their own income and utility, subject to certain limitations which economists refer to as "externalities". One of these, for example, is that you should not pollute your environment. As soon as these conditions are met, I do believe that such value maximising systems would indeed lead to the "Wealth of Nations", as in the title of Adam Smith's book. As far as my own work is concerned, I believe everyone should attempt to maximise the value for the shareholders. Everyone should determine for themselves which companies are likely to do the best. But we live in an uncertain world. No one knows which companies are priced too high and for that reason the individual investor should concern himself with both the risk and the profit. And my theory provides the answer here.'

Even though senior management talk of little other than maximising shareholder value, do the measures taken to this end really address this matter? Is a true value-creating strategy really applied?

Prof. Markowitz: 'Managers are also people and they have their own objectives. If, in order to achieve those objectives, they do not look at the interests of the shareholders, then they run the risk of being replaced by managers who sufficiently care about the shareholders.'

What is your opinion on the recent developments on the financial market? Do you think all the events are the result of a lack of strategic vision in the financial world? Is there a breach between the financial market and economic reality?

Prof. Markowitz: 'I think the world is best served by the free circulation of capital. The world is an uncertain place and we spread out investments in an attempt to diminish that uncertainty to a certain extent. If you try to diversify your portfolio, then theory states that your most important worry should be how many things go up or go down at the same time. You should be worried about the covariances. These covariances change over time. The world changes and our own deeds change the world. The world today is more strongly interlinked and in the case of certain panic situations we see that the covariances are higher that we originally thought. Therefore, in analysing our portfolio, we should be asking ourselves whether we are dealing with variability and covariances "from year to year", under normal circumstances; or whether we are dealing with covariances "from day to day" which you sometimes find in a panic situation. Which combination you prefer depends on the type of investor you are. If you only take long positions and have a long-term view, then the long-term fluctuations should worry you. But if you have high "leverage" and you stick your neck out, then day-to-day fluctuations can wipe you out.'

Is it socially acceptable that the short term view – say for about one month – can influence the system of the entire financial world?

Prof. Markowitz: 'We should have learned from the events surrounding Long Term Capital Management (LTCM). The banks were prepared to increase their credit without knowing exactly how much credit had already been granted. The lesson was clear: banks must ensure they have better information. If I understand it correctly, the LTCM "hedges" were a combination of long positions in low quality instruments and short positions in high quality instruments. What happened was that the low quality instruments took a blow and the high quality instruments took off. In addition, "leverage" was extremely high. Because something always worked a certain way in the past, it doesn't mean to say that things won't change in the future.'

What kind of future do you expect? Will it be a future full of statistics and IT; in other words a future without a soul?

Prof. Markowitz: 'There should be a division of labour between theory and judgement: on the one hand because of the gaps in our theories and on the other hand because of the shortcomings of the human mind. As far as the latter is concerned, if I were to give you a list of securities and ask you to find the best combination for minimising the risks, you would find it very difficult to do so. This is where computers come into their own, but they are not good at reading what a top executive has to say on new plans, or at determining the risk of the organisation getting into difficulties. In general, this is something analysts do better. What we need is a division of tasks between the understanding analyst and the calculating computer.'

Do you think there is a difference between financial management at strategic level and financial management at operational level?

Prof. Markowitz: 'The way things are frequently done in American pension funds is that at a high level they analyse the types of assets and determine how much they should invest in each type. Buying securities is the responsibility of "stock pickers". When I was writing my book, I originally thought that you went straight from your expectations to acquiring individual securities. Managers who are focused on quantitative analysis sometimes do it that way and others approach things with the help of strategic planning. This seems to me to be a reasonable approach.'

Do you have a special message for the business community in the Netherlands and for accountants and students in this country?

Prof. Markowitz: 'Accounting figures are the substance of the information process. We are information processors; if we didn't have accountants, then we wouldn't have any information to process. We are really interested in the future, but all information originates in the past. You can use the past to help predict the future by analysing how well you would have done if you had taken a particular decision and what the result would have been if you had assumed one figure instead of another.

Controllers and economics students must understand that in this world there is a division of tasks between people who are a little more skilled at calculating, but who are prepared to listen to and work with others who know the actual practical situation, and people who specialise in practical situations, but who know where to go when they have analysis questions.'

6. A personal vision on the future of finance

In conversation with Professor M.H. Miller

Professor Merton Miller was born in 1923 and was awarded his first degree by Harvard University in 1943. In 1952, he gained a PhD from the Johns Hopkins University and now has a total of about eight honorary degrees from various universities, both in the US and abroad. He has taught at the Carnegie Mellon University and has been attached to the University of Chicago since 1961 where he is currently distinguished service professor emeritus. In 1990, he became Nobel Laureate in Economics for his fundamental contributions to the theory of corporate finance.

Prof. M.H. Miller

The topic of the book in which this interview will be published is 'Strategic Finance'. How do you define the concept?

Prof. Miller: 'In my definition I try to make a distinction between what I call "Strategic" Finance and "Tactical" Finance. The same distinction can also be made between what I call the Business School approach to finance and the Economics department approach to finance. The Business School approach is what I call tactical finance, which is concerned with optimisation, optimal portfolio theory, optimal capital structures, optimal dividend policy and so on. This is the decision-making side of finance, whereas to me strategic finance is the study of the capital market; you try to explain how the capital markets work and why things are what they are. Strategic finance is a branch of economics whereas tactical finance is teaching people how to do things. Business Schools teach people to run firms and to manage portfolios etc., so they place a lot of emphasis on short-term tactical manoeuvres. The difference between the two concepts is the difference between "macro" and "micro".'

Do you believe in managing a company only on the basis of shareholder value and value based management? What about the other stakeholders in a company, are they less important?

Prof. Miller: 'There is nothing new in the concept of maximising shareholder value. Back in 1970 when Eugene Fama and I wrote a textbook on the theory of finance it was clear that maximising shareholder value was something that you had to do as an economist. There is nothing mysterious about maximising shareholder value. As for the other stakeholders, I don't think that corporate management should do anything except work for the stockholders.

The textbook theories I developed over the years with Eugene Fama and other theorists have been applied by others in business settings. The beauty of what Joel Stern and others have done with concepts like economic value added (EVA) is to explain them to businessmen in terms that they can understand. We on the other hand were primarily addressing an academic audience, not a business audience. It's been up to the EVA people to translate these academic notions into operational terms for a business. Economic value added is superior to the more traditional concepts of return on equity and return on investment because the latter easily drift off into mistaken behaviour. Value added covers everything; it judges the firm on the basis of the capital it uses. So many of these other criteria, which I call "pseudo criteria", lead to a maximisation of the wrong things and not to a maximisation of shareholder value. They permit wrong decisions and sometimes even permit managers to maximise their own reward, even though this isn't compatible with the stockholders' best interests.'

Could you give your opinion on the propositions developed 41 years ago by yourself and Modigliani? What have been the practical consequences of the propositions for financial management?

Prof. Miller: 'Perhaps, I could start by briefly explaining the main point of our first proposition. It stated that in an economist's ideal world of complete and perfect capital markets and with full and symmetric information among all market participants, the total market value of all the securities issued by a company was dictated by the earning power and risk of its underlying real assets and was independent of how the mix of securities issued to finance it was divided between debt instruments and equity capital. The analogy we originally used was the company as an enormous vat of milk. The farmer could sell the milk as it is or separate off the cream and sell it at a much higher price than the original milk. This is analogous to a company selling low-yield and thus high-priced debt securities. Once the cream is removed, however, the skimmed milk remaining would sell for much less than the original milk. This is analogous to the levered equity. Our first proposition was that if there were no separation costs (and no government subsidies), the cream plus the skimmed milk would have the same price as the original milk.

You must remember, however, that our propositions were not developed for practical businessmen, but for academics. Because the propositions are basically correct in the way they describe the operation of the capital market they have a lot of relevance for business, if businesses want to look at them. Let me give you one example of relevance that you may not be aware of. In the USA, there are currently a number of law suits being pursued in which savings and loans associations, which were affected by some changes in the law that the federal government made in 1989, are suing the Federal Government for damages. The Modigliani/Miller propositions have figured very prominently in these cases because of the nature of the litigation. The Government insisted that these saving banks had to have a higher capital ratio, and these banks are now saying that they were not allowed to leverage as much as they wanted to. The Modigliani/Miller propositions state therefore that leverage isn't worth anything so they are very much part of this litigation. Clearly, the practical consequences have been enormous. When you ask about the effect of the Modigliani/Miller propositions on financial managers, I honestly believe that most will not have heard of them, but they are nevertheless talking our lingo, even though they probably do not know where the ideas came from.'

You can't consistently beat a simple index of stock prices. Underlying this is a belief in an efficient financial market. But behavioural finance theorists disagree. What is your opinion about this discussion and about behavioural finance in general?

Prof. Miller: 'Well I'm completely behind Professor Fama on this; I don't think that the efficient market theory has been shaken much. There are always anomalies, but I don't think anybody has demonstrated any serious flaws. I personally have mixed feelings about the behavioural people. A lot of young people concerned with finance want to make a mark in the field that is now already quite mature and so they have branched out into new areas, one of which is behavioural finance. I don't think it's going anywhere. We don't really need much in the way of the psychology of choice for the propositions that we are concerned with. I am an economist and I believe we should leave psychology to the psychologists. I do not believe that behavioural finance has any contribution to make when you are dealing with the kind of problems that I call strategic finance.'

Derivatives and corporate risk management: a dangerous game in the eyes of a lot of people. What is your opinion? In the Orange County and the Metallgesellschaft cases is it fair to say that it was not the derivatives but the accountants that were the problem?

Prof. Miller: 'Orange County had very little to do with derivatives. It was strictly a question of leverage. They were borrowing short term and lending long term and they ran into organisational difficulties about that, but everything would have turned out fine if they had been left alone. Orange County was neither insolvent nor illiquid. Metallgesellschaft is a much more complicated issue. Its problem was a managerial problem and not one of derivatives. The management had problems understanding the situation and had objectives of its own. Some people suspect that the supervisory board provoked the crisis so that they could get rid of the management. One of the hardest managerial decisions you have to make is when to cut off an operation that's profitable in the long run but is losing money in the short run. In my opinion, derivatives often get the blame because they are rather new and poorly understood. In all of the cases that I have looked at, and there have been many more than just these two, there is usually some kind of managerial mistake involved. Take Barings, for example. The firm was set up in such a way that if there hadn't been a Nick Leeson there would have been somebody else. The fact of the matter was that Barings had poor management controls.'

What is your opinion about the mergers in the financial world? Are global financial institutions still under control? Do we need a kind of 'United Nations' for the financial world (and taxes on financial flows)?

Prof. Miller: 'That is the current cliché at the moment, but I have always argued that governments wouldn't know what to do anyway and they usually intervene to protect some of their own constituents. I don't see that they contribute anything and I don't see that there is any disconnect between the financial markets and the real world. I am not worried at all about these mergers; if they are profitable they will take place, if they are not profitable they will be unwound. I think it's good that the governments can't control everything because they would only make things worse. Central banks also cause a lot of trouble; they don't solve anything. In Europe, you could say that the great advantage of the European Central Bank is that there is now only one central bank, while there used to be eleven. Even a single global central bank would be a dreadful mistake; the best thing for a government to do is nothing! I don't say that there shouldn't be prudential limits of some kind on banks, but we don't need a world monetary authority. That would be a disaster.

If you look at the financial crisis in Asia, you see that companies have been far too bank-driven and have been making investments for reasons other than maximising shareholder value, so the problems eventually caught up with them. My advice to all involved in such a situation is very simple. Maximise profit. Do what is profitable and not what is trendy. Do not be worried about the opinions of other people. If there is a profitable opportunity take it, although this is hard in such countries because many do not have a very strong rule of law. The problems will only be solved when the Asian countries are put on a normal economic basis where firms and banks are run for profit and not for state objectives or to help out friends or the local autocrats.'

Many people say that financial markets are driven by IT (the Internet etc.). Is a complete rupture between financial and real markets dangerous?
Prof. Miller: 'No, I've lived for a long time and I've seen that that's the way progress goes. New things keep emerging and they wouldn't emerge unless they satisfied a need. The Internet is spreading very rapidly because it provides certain important services at lower costs than the present methods do. I don't see any threat at all. IT provides a method for accessing the market that is merely an extension of the way things were done in the past. IT will have implications for many fields. For instance, we in the academic field are a very high cost way of providing educational services and I think these new developments of the Internet and electronic instruction are going to make inroads into traditional academic arrangements. There is no doubt that costs will be lowered. I don't think we are going to eliminate all the professors overnight or anything like that, but a lot of operations can probably be taken over by the computer.'

What are for you the hot topics in finance for the coming years?
Prof. Miller: 'Well, as I mentioned earlier I think that finance is a quite mature subject area, I don't see much new development except for one important area. The real big news about finance in the last twenty years has been the development of Option theory. There's an enormous

amount still to be done at the micro level and in extending options into new areas. At the macro level the most striking thing I'd like to point out is that thanks to derivatives and options and so on, risk is moving away from the original sources and spreading into the whole community. Let me give you a few examples. The biggest news in banking is what is referred to as "credit derivatives". By using credit derivatives, risks that used to be taken by the banks are now put out into the capital market so that everybody can buy a piece of them. Another development is weather derivatives; in the future there will be disaster futures which will lead to the insurance industry moving much closer to the rest of the financial world. The spread of risk sharing techniques is going to be enormous and I think this is going to lead to a change in emphasis in the way the field is mostly taught these days. The option notion is going to spread throughout the field of finance.

The global trend that's important is the spread of risk sharing throughout the whole capital market, no longer just in terms of traditional securities but also in terms of the new developments mentioned above.'

What is the most important message that you give to your students at the Chicago Business School?

Prof. Miller: 'I tell my students to be sure to study options; options are everywhere, and options are going to be, both intellectually and practically, a major part of the field of finance. There will have to be a lot of emphasis on asset pricing, but options are essential and the field is tremendously complicated and extensive. Not only finance students, but also other professionals will have to start reading about options.'

Finally, what is your opinion about corporate governance; is it a really important issue for you?

Prof. Miller: 'I think the world is beginning to move towards the American way of doing things, which is to focus on maximising shareholder value and thus create efficiency in that way. I think it is good that Europe is copying the American way in this respect and putting less focus on banking.'

7. Going Far East: dangers and challenges

In conversation with Mr. J. Lintjer

In the Netherlands we have already known for centuries that as soon as the locks are closed, the water in canals, channels, reaches and watercourses is no longer renewed. If it is not refreshed for a long period this obviously has an influence on the quality of the water. As soon as it can be drained again, this will have new impulses for the life in and on the water. This is no different from the locations that have to handle flows of money, goods and services every day: the markets. Those who close off their markets for fear of a flow from outside are sooner or later confronted with stagnation. Are countries that opt for an open policy rewarded for this?

Mr. J. Lintjer

'Absolutely, as soon as you propagate an open economy – more trade, more exports, more imports, more life – you also gain much easier access to new technologies and new ideas. The Asian Development Bank has conducted a study into the growth and blossoming of Asian economies during the period 1965 to 1990. It appeared from this that "open" economies have yearly experienced 2% more growth than economies which have pursued the "protectionist" line.'

These are the words of John Lintjer (1943), since January 1999 Vice-President of the Executive Board of the Asian Development Bank and previously chairman of the OECD Privatisation advisory body.

What is the role of the Asian Development Bank compared to that of the other international institutions, such as the IMF and the World Bank?

Mr. Lintjer: 'Our bank is a regional development bank, a multilateral development institution which focuses exclusively on Asia and the

Pacific. The IMF is global and focuses especially on the recovery of macroeconomic and balance of payments imbalances and on financial stability. The World Bank also operates globally. In this respect it does exactly the same as the Asian Development Bank, i.e. makes structured contributions to the long-term development of developing countries by means of specific lending programmes and by means of direct loans. In addition, it also provides technical assistance in the same way that we do.

With this more structural approach, the World Bank and the Asian Development Bank try to support the IMF's macroeconomic stabilisation role. Compared to the World Bank, the Asian Development Bank has the advantage that it is not only a multilateral bank like the World Bank (countries both inside and outside the region are shareholders), but also that it has an Asian character.

We work closely together with the Asian countries at all levels: at country level, at sector level, at project level. We are free from political interference and provide advice in consultation. We do not pretend to have all the wisdom at our disposal. As a non-Asian I also notice that the people from our bank are extremely welcome in all Asian countries because we give advice at their level and do not try to dictate matters. Our recommendations are not regarded as foreign interference in domestic affairs, while the IMF and World Bank are regarded rather more as typical western institutions.'

The bank can thus be compared to the European Investment Bank (EIB), while is regional after all?

Mr. Lintjer: 'I think the best comparison is the East European Bank, the Interamerican Development Bank for Latin America and the African Development Bank for Africa. In my opinion, that is a better comparison because these banks also have non-regional shareholders. Ninety percent of the EIB's activities are in and for the EU member states and you can't really call them all development projects.'

In July 1997, the 'Asian miracle' was turned upside down; what went wrong exactly?

Mr. Lintjer: 'Various explanations can be given. In my opinion, the main reason is that the Southeast Asian countries were not sufficiently prepared for their new role on the world stage. The centralised development model of these countries with an authoritarian and risk-taking government could not tolerate global market liberalisation at the end of the day. They clearly had problems with the fact that the world market has its own divergent rules. Furthermore, they find the process of financial integration on the global scale hard to swallow.

With respect to the "Asian miracle" you refer to, it certainly was a wonder that was caused by big investments. On average, they were more than 30% of GNP. The Asian countries have also placed considerable reliance on their export potential. Export income was used to a great extent to import technology. When you combine this with a high level of schooling in the countries in question (more than 50% of children are registered for secondary school), this means that they have utilised their possibilities well. We also quickly saw this in their economic results. If we look at a 30-year period (from 1968 to 1997) – thus up until the start of the crisis – we see that the Southeast Asian countries had an average GNP growth of 6.6%, while the global average was 3.8%. During these years the European countries continually had budgetary deficits, while the Southeast Asian countries had government savings averaging about 3.5% of GNP. You can only deduce from this that the macroeconomic policy in these countries was very good. Fiscal and monetary policy was very prudent; there were no deficits in the state coffers like there were in Europe. So the cause of the Asian crisis does not lie in the field of macroeconomic policy.'

Nevertheless, the world was startled by a crisis that started in the middle of 1997 and that resulted in fairly high negative growth figures in the countries in question. In 1998, Thailand had negative growth of 1%, the Philippines fell by 6.2%, Malaysia by 8% and Indonesia by almost 14%. What were the negative effects?

Mr. Lintjer: 'The Asian countries took out more and more foreign loans in the nineteen nineties. Foreign financing became very important. In countries like Korea and Thailand, the average debt/equity ratio in companies in 1996 was more than 200%; in 1999 this figure even increased to the intolerable leverage ratio of 400% or more. The same development occurred, although with lower percentages, in Indonesia, the Philippines and Hong Kong.

Another aspect is that where there was a pegged exchange rate between foreign currencies and the US dollar, domestic financial parties thought that they could borrow without any exchange risk. They were too optimistic in their assessment. The interest rate differential with countries outside the region was fairly large and so international investors looked for possibilities to invest with a higher return.

Furthermore, the expectations for the future of the Asian economies were exaggerated. That is also why too much was borrowed. After

1990, the total amount of loans by countries like Malaysia and Thailand practically doubled. It was actually in 1996 that things first went wrong. Exports decreased, mainly in the field of electronics, and this represents no less than half of total exports. In 1996, there was an overcapacity on the world market in that area. The dollar rose with the local currencies following suit as a result of the exchange pegging and that contributed even more to the slowdown in export growth. One thing led to another. People became worried about the exchange rates, became sceptical about growth potential and, as a result, the substantial inflow of foreign capital was threatened. The exchange rates came under pressure. This had a serious negative effect on the balance sheets of banks and other companies, at least insofar as they had not hedged their foreign currency loans, and in general they hadn't because of the exchange peg.

Foreign investors then got into a panic. If we take the five more seriously affected countries, Singapore, Indonesia, Malaysia, Philippines and Thailand, and examine the net capital flows, we see that in 1996 there was still a net private capital inflow of 105 billion dollars while in 1997/1998 there was a net private capital outflow of about 30 billion dollars, thus a major exodus of capital amounting to about 12% of GNP. The system was unable to absorb such a blow.'

Why the panic?

Mr. Lintjer: 'Foreign investors started to realise that in the years before 1996 an enormous amount of capital had flown in and that, as a result, it was very difficult to allocate it efficiently with a view to healthy earnings performance. There were three kinds of imbalances in the financial structure. First of all, there was a miscalculation about the amount of funds available to pay the nominal value of bonds to their holders on the requisite date: the maturity mismatch. Assets and liabilities deviated from one another. Short-term foreign loans were used to finance long-term domestic projects. Naturally, things go wrong when problems occur.

The second miscalculation was the currency mismatch: the value of loans was expressed in foreign currencies, while the loan itself was provided in local currencies. Things went wrong because the exchange rates came under pressure.

Thirdly, there was the credit risk mismatch: credit was very easy to obtain and, as a result, the analysis about which investments were actually healthy and produced return was poor. Investments were made in much riskier assets, such as real estate, shares and the like, than was wise.

Well, the combination of these three miscalculations meant that the financial position of banks and other companies became extremely vulnerable.

During the past 30 years, we observed that there was a close relationship in the Asian countries between government, banks and companies. In the Asian development model governments play a central policy role in the field of industry and services, both by means of the allocation of resources and by means of the (implicit) issue of guarantees. Investments were co-ordinated in consultation with the banks that acted as financing medium. We once enviously regarded that as a strong structure, but it now appears that this is a weak point. We now see that legislation and regulations in those countries are inadequate. It is now striking that governments do not pursue a transparent policy so that non-transparent debt ratios arise. They do not have independent supervisory bodies like we do here. They do not have properly working accounting standards and the like. And it also appears that the banks lent money too easily on account of insufficiently strict prudential supervision by the central bank. To put it briefly, the cause of the crisis was not macroeconomic mismanagement, but inadequacies in the financial structures. Therefore, we do not refer to a current account crisis, but to a capital account crisis which has also led to serious domestic credit contraction.'

Like some Noble prizewinners, you argue in favour of rather more control of international capital flows so that the world is not plunged into a crisis from one day to the next?

Mr. Lintjer: 'Yes, but for a very limited group of countries. Restrictions with respect to the movements of capital are particularly necessary for those countries which opened their capital account without first implementing the necessary structural reforms. In general, these countries do not have a properly functioning capital market, hardly a bond market. Financing is effected only by banks and they do not have transparent markets.

Well, one of the lessons from the Asian crisis could be to look rather more carefully into the possibilities of gradually opening the capital account, depending upon the absorption capacity and the utilisation policy of the country itself. However, one should also be careful with this: if the capital account is not completely opened up, the problem of short capital movements arises. As a consequence, the country becomes extremely sensitive to the movements of the investors. Such a step should certainly not be rushed. The fact that China has not been affected by the crisis is because the capital accounts are kept closed in that area, and that is a very wise move as long as the domestic structure is not modified. We would also advise India to do that: open the capital account gradually and not in one fell swoop.'

How will the Asian system develop after this crisis?

Mr. Lintjer: 'The financial sector is going through a process of reorientation. The emphasis now lies on the development of the capital market because that was the cause of the crisis. A second element is that the banking industry's non-performing loans have increased substantially, both as a result of the crisis and the credit contraction. Solutions must be found for this. The financial sector will have to be restructured at the expense of shareholders and taxpayers. Furthermore, there will have to be more room for supervision and the financial infrastructure will have to grow. The most fundamental change is a new evaluation of the Asian "managed development" model that has traditionally been employed by governments and banks.

This evaluation is vital. As a result of the crisis, the governments have started stimulating liberalisation and the deregulation of the financial sector. Greater emphasis is now placed on the independence of the central bank, on commercialisation and on competing markets. More attention is being given to the development of the capital market as source of finance instead of leaving this role to the banks. The restructuring of the financial sector will therefore have to be accompanied by a reorganisation of the banking industry. This means closures, mergers and acquisitions and access to the local financial markets for foreign banks. This process will certainly be substantiated further and I don't think that is a bad thing.

The Basle Accords concerning capital adequacy ratios have actually never been applied in Asia, but that will certainly take place now. A classification system for borrowers will also be developed, something that was not thought necessary because money was lent to friends and acquaintances. Risks will certainly be examined more closely.'

So what you are saying is that what we consider quite normal in the west – regulation of the financial sector, a properly controlled banking sector, adequate risk management and suchlike – has never caught on in Asia?

Mr. Lintjer: 'That's right, in combination with the fact that legislation and regulations did not come up to the mark. If a company was threatened with bankruptcy, it was practically impossible for debtors to recoup their losses. The process of taking bankruptcy cases to court with which we are familiar in the west does not exist there. Bankruptcy legislation is not properly developed, if it already exists at all. You see, there is nothing the matter as long as the economy is doing well. As long as you can continue driving, you don't need any brakes. But woe betide you if there is an enormous setback. Only then is it apparent whether the system is functioning properly. Fortunately, we now see that the relationship between government, financial sector and business community is changing. This not only means that companies are choosing a new strategy, but also that corporate governance is starting to play an important role, with a greater role for internal control and financial reporting. Companies will have to examine their capital structure more than they did previously.'

What role does governance play?

Mr. Lintjer: 'I would like to regard governance as the way in which power is used and this differs enormously from country to country. Four characteristics can be distinguished in governance. The first is accountability. People and institutions must be made accountable for their actions and must also be able to justify them. There must be sanctions to exact accountability.

The second characteristic is transparency. It is especially important to obtain reliable and timely information that is also understandable. I sometimes see statistics here that may look impressive, but actually say nothing to me. Information must be reliable and meaningful.

A third characteristic of governance is the predictability and certainty. As an entrepreneur, investor or involved party you have got to know where you stand. What do we now see in many countries? We see that the legislation and the rules are not clear about what can be expected of them. This scares off investors, of course. Rules must be implemented in a uniform and effective manner. My competitor must not be treated any differently to the way I am in the same situation.

The fourth characteristic is participation, support. There must be sufficient support among large sections of the population for what a government, a company or an organisation wants to achieve. As Asian Development Bank we have quite a lot of contact with community-based groups that have particular ideas about changes in society, but which are not shared by the government.

Another important aspect is freedom of the press and democracy, although I should be reticent about this because the Asian Development Bank is not concerned with the political structure in a country.

Nevertheless, the fact is that freedom of the press is bound up with transparency, and democracy with the broadening of public support. And so I once again return to the characteristics of governance.

When we talk about governance in Europe, we very quickly think about shareholder value, the reinforcement of the role of the shareholder. In Asia, people's concept of it is more basic. We talk about the transparent management of scarce resources. Governance can mean that the credibility of the capital market is increased and this also means that savers must be encouraged to get their money out from under the mattress or out of an old sock and invest it. That capital is badly needed to develop the economy. By the way, mergers and acquisitions will also play an important role. In the past, companies have in fact given a higher priority to a purely quantitative expansion of their activities, their sales volume and their market share. The latter is actually looked at more than earnings performance. One hopes that this will change dramatically in the aftermath of the crisis.'

So the minds are not yet completely ready for this?
Mr. Lintjer: 'That varies from country to country and from political system to political system. The South Korean government, for example, is now extremely busy changing the economy in that sense and thus society as well. It is trying to pull apart the system, currently dominated by five major conglomerates, and make it more transparent. The providers of capital will then at least know what risks are faced. The government and the president are doing very good work in this respect.

If I may go one step further: there is even a risk that they will lose political support for these fundamental changes as soon as the economy grows again in accordance with the familiar cycles. As a result, the politicians or the population may go back to sleep – things are getting better again, so why the changes – and real changes will fail to materialise. The price will then be enormous if the economy subsequently nose-dives.

Nevertheless, desperate diseases require desperate remedies. The undoubtedly unpopular measures will initially lead to make changes in society in the short term: higher unemployment, for instance. This may lead a government that is not very sure of itself to refrain from making the absolutely essential interventions and so nothing is solved at the end of the day.

The crisis has enormous consequences in the social arena. In the nineteen nineties, the number of people in Asia living in absolute poverty (defined as income of $1 per day) decreased by more than 100 million, although this has increased again by a few score millions because of the financial crisis. It is estimated that there are currently more than 900 million poor living on the Asian continent. Households that could afford to send their children to school have now withdrawn them so that they can earn some money and thus supplement the family income. We estimate that six million children in Indonesia were taken out of school because family income was too low. These children have now returned to the street to beg or sell. This makes itself felt in the future: these children become tomorrow's unskilled unemployed. That is one of the major social problems of this crisis. It is a crisis that actually costs an entire generation. As Asian Development Bank we feel very strongly about preventing poverty. In the example of Indonesia we have therefore started many projects at the local level in order to get the street-children back into the schools.'

Is the patient on the mend?

Mr. Lintjer: 'Yes, he is getting better. We are seeing a slight improvement this year. Korea is recovering more quickly than Indonesia. The support provided by the international community clearly appears to be having some success. On this continent, Japan continues to play a particularly important role. We expect a lot from the fiscal stimuli – we are talking about 135 billion dollars – which should give the economy a push. However, a lot also depends upon what happens in the US. That country has had high growth for many years, but a recession cannot be precluded. Since about 21% of the exports from Asia are absorbed by the US, a slowing down of growth there will have an immediate effect. This is surprisingly less the case for Japan and also Europe that account for 12% and 15% of the exports respectively. Incidentally, the most important component is the intra-regional trade (50%), which points to considerable interdependence.'

So within two years we will see a fundamental improvement and not a superficial, spurious solution based on semi state-controlled funding?

Mr. Lintjer: 'That is certainly what I expect. However, I would make the reservation that the fundamental restructuring operations should be continued within the economy. After all, the restructuring process is not even half, and perhaps only a quarter complete. So it is essential that the process is continued and persevered with. In November 1998, Japan announced a 24 trillion yen reflationary package for the year 1999. In dollar terms, this is no less than 200 billion for this period alone.'

As European banker, what would you advise the European entrepreneur who is currently active or who wants to be active on the Asian market? Should he withdraw completely, maintain his current position or await developments?

Mr. Lintjer: 'If I were a European businessman I wouldn't neglect my interests in the Asian market. The Asian crisis has passed its peak and slight economic growth has replaced economic contraction. Insofar as the Stock Price Index can provide an indication for economic growth, we are now quite clearly seeing an increase in share prices. We are now also seeing new foreign companies very cautiously entering the region, although I should add that some foreign companies are also leaving it. Nevertheless, there are now some interesting opportunities for our entrepreneurs. Of course, if I want to do business I must take risks. Focused investment in Asia is a healthy risk.'

Do you expect to see a development whereby US and European companies and banks start to run the show in Asian countries?

Mr. Lintjer: 'No, I don't believe that will be the case. Ten years ago, we thought that Japanese banks would take over our banks, companies and real estate. But things did not go that way. Nor do I believe that European and American companies will now absorb Asian companies en masse. First of all, I believe that Asian companies and governments will continue with the process of reform and that the economy will be structurally strengthened as a result. Countries and companies that want to be successful in the global economy cannot afford to revert to the cosy non-transparent domestic relationships of the past. The process of opening up economies that led to a 30-year period of flourishing growth will not be stopped by the Asian crisis (despite the serious effects). Most of the afflicted economies will, with possible ups and downs, adapt to the demands of the global economy. Young generations of entrepreneurs and policymakers take a pride in having their countries grow and having them play a role in the global economy. In this process, achievements such as good governance, transparency and reliable legislation and regulations will little by little become a structured and accepted element of society. This has two effects. Firstly, these countries will eventually emerge more strongly from the financial crisis and thus also compete more intensely with other countries. But secondly, the process of adjustment will provide great opportunities for our business community, particularly in the area of direct investment. If Europe gets involved with an expected Asian revival in good time, it will also benefit from impulses for its own healthy economic development.'

8. A visit to the European Union's financing institution

In conversation with Mr. R.W. de Korte

The European Investment Bank (EIB), with its seat in Luxembourg, was established in 1958. The bank was given the task of providing loans for capital investment projects to support the realisation of European policy objectives. The emphasis in this respect is regional development, Trans-European Networks (TENs) in transport, telecommunications and energy, the enhancement of the international competitiveness and the integration of European industry, the stimulation of investments by small and medium-sized enterprises (SMEs), environmental protection and securing energy supplies. The bank has grown and it is now also active outside the European Union within the framework of the Union's development and co-operation policy.

Mr. R.W. de Korte

In addition, the European Investment Bank participates in a public-private partnership: the European Investment Fund (EIF). This was established in 1994 by the EIB, the European Community and private and public financial institutions from the member states of the European Union. The Fund provides credit guarantees for TENs and SMEs and supplies venture capital. The EIF acts as a catalyst: it stimulates the partnership with the private sector in TENs projects and it participates in venture capital funds for innovative SMEs.

The shareholders of the EIB are the member states of the European Union, which all participate in the bank's capital. They are represented on the EIB's Board of Governors by a minister, normally the Minister of Finance. The Briton Sir Brian Unwin has been president of the bank since 1993 and the Dutchman Rudolf de Korte is vice-president. The unpaid part of the bank's subscribed capital serves as guarantee capital that can be called up as required to comply with the bank's obligations. The EIB raises its funds on the capital markets where it has an excellent reputation (AAA-rating).

Rudolf de Korte (1936) studied mathematics and physics and also took his doctoral degree in these subjects. Following a Business School course, he entered the world of marketing. He worked for Shell in the Far East and in East Africa and, on account of his interest in marketing, subsequently became director of a Unilever subsidiary in the 1970s. In addition, he was secretary of the Dutch liberal VVD political party for a number of years. When he was asked to put up for political office, he did so after serious thought and became deputy Prime Minister and Minister of Economic Affairs.

The result of this was that he has served in two Cabinets and subsequently in the Opposition. He has been a Supervisory Board Member of several companies. In 1995, he became vice-president of the European Investment Bank on the recommendation of the Dutch government.

Where should the EIB be situated within the institutional order of the European Union?

Mr. De Korte: 'The EIB has its own role in the Treaty of Rome and the Treaty of Amsterdam. We are an autonomous body of the European Union with our own decision-making bodies. Mr. Duisenberg's ECB has been given a role in the Treaty of Amsterdam in a similar way to ours. While the ECB is the monetary authority, we are the principal banker for long-term financing operations in the European Union and, under certain conditions, are also active outside it.

We work closely together with the European Commission, but we are not part of it as is sometimes mistakenly thought. The Commission's director-general of Economic and Financial Affairs (DG-II) has a seat on the bank's Board of Directors and is thus one of our directors. Loans are approved by the Board of Directors, under the authority of the Board of Governors, the bank's highest body. The Board of Directors is the non-executive body with which the executive Management Committee, of which I am a member, constantly communicates. Decisions prepared by us are submitted to the Board of Directors for approval.

Where our co-operation with the European Commission is concerned, we for instance deploy European Union budget resources although mainly loans from our own resources. We mainly work together with the Commission with respect to financing under the EU's Structural Funds and the Cohesion Fund in order to stimulate the Union's regional development areas. These grant funds are often accompanied by our loans, which are in fact comparable with commercial loans, but often have very long terms. Our tariff structure is not very much different, sometimes slightly more competitive than those for commercial loans. In any case, we are obliged to cover the costs. In other words, our bank is not an institution that does not provide subsidies.'

Why is the public in the Netherlands not very familiar with the EIB?
Mr. De Korte: 'The European Investment Bank was established to accelerate the economic integration of less favoured regions within the Community, initially particularly in the south of Italy. As much as 50% of the Bank's portfolio was Italian and a complete operational entity still exists in Rome. In other words, the Bank was established to foster balanced development of the former European Community and today's European Union. Our focus was and still is the poorer regions.

Half of the of the European Union's citizens still live in less favoured regions and that is mainly where the Bank deploys most of its lending activities. The Portuguese and the Greeks know the EIB very well. In the Netherlands, it is mainly the financiers, the savers, the investors and the pension funds who know what the Bank does, but sure enough the average citizen doesn't. In the Netherlands, the EIB mainly absorbs savings funds. In this sense, the bank has proven its worth for the Dutch capital market. In 1961, the Bank's very first borrowing operation involved the guilder on the Dutch capital market. In the 1970s and 1980s, the borrowing operations in the Netherlands increased to about 15% of the total external capital raised by the Bank. This has now decreased again because other markets offer better borrowing opportunities. For instance, we now make a lot of use of markets like that of New York (the dollar market), the Swiss market, the Tokyo market (the yen market) etc. The Dutch market is still important, also in connection with the development of the euro. The first operation performed by the bank in the "euro tributary issues" category was in guilders at the beginning of 1997. This means that the loan was originally issued in guilders in the Netherlands. When the real euro appeared on the scene, this loan was redenominated as were similar loans which had been issued since then in other currencies. Since the introduction of the euro, such loans are denominated in euros. The interesting thing about this technique was that the individual loans were amalgamated into a few large loans. This concept was thus first launched in the Netherlands in January 1997. The Dutch capital market was therefore once again important for us because it was able to test such a product.

The largest borrowing operation in a national currency to be performed by the Bank was also launched in the Netherlands in 1996. This entailed the raising of 2.5 billion guilders in one go.

Returning to the subject of the very first euro tributary issue, this was an innovative structure that aimed as it were to structure our euro capital market operations with the future in mind. This pioneering work has become a success. Whereas Dutch citizens may not know us so well, the Dutch capital market has always been important for the EIB. On the lending side, on the other hand, the Netherlands is under the European average. The Netherlands has a participation in the Bank's share capital of almost 5%, but the percentage share of our lending operations in the Netherlands is usually lower than this.'

What are the differences between what the European Bank for Reconstruction and Development (EBRD) and the EIB do?

Mr. De Korte: 'The EIB is the financing institution of the European Union and is a real investment bank: longer term, large projects. 75% of our lending is in infrastructure. The EBRD belongs to the group of multilateral development banks, such as the World Bank. Incidentally, the EIB holds a 3% stake in the EBRD and our president is a governor of the EBRD, so there is a connection.

The EBRD is also active in those regions where we are not present, for instance in the former Soviet Union.

The future EU member states are an important field of operation for the EIB, a situation that is comparable to that in Spain, Portugal and Greece before they joined the Union. In these three member states the Bank also played an important role in the development of the domestic capital markets. We are now repeating this in Eastern Europe.'

Is the EIB organised in such a way that it is managed as a private institution?

Mr. De Korte: 'In that respect we can afford to be rather proud of ourselves. The EIB only has 1000 staff. So it is clear that we work effectively. We do not attempt to make a profit and we do not pay taxes. We are a financial institution that operates on a cost-plus basis, but we do ensure that our operations eventually produce a surplus. This surplus is needed to guarantee our continuity. We are of the opinion that there must be a return on our own funds and strive for a return that corresponds with the long-term bond interest rate over a period of five to six years. That is our yardstick. Insofar as we can add reserves to our net assets, we can grow without the member states having to cough up new capital.'

How is the strategy determined and what is the strategy at the moment for the capital increase in the medium term?

Mr. De Korte: 'The Board of Governors has approved an increase in the subscribed capital of EIB from 62 billion to 100 billion euro. The increase came into effect on 1 January 1999 and that gives us enough leeway for at least the coming five years. With subscribed capital of 100 billion euro, EIB's statutory lending ceiling is 250 billion euro, i.e. 250% of the subscribed capital. At the end of 1998, the total of loans outstanding was 155 billion euro. The capital contribution is set at 6% of the subscribed capital and the increase is, as I just explained, financed from EIB's own reserves. The paid-up capital thus increased from 4.7 billion to 6 billion euros.

The capital increase was becoming necessary because at the request of the European Union the Bank is faced with new tasks. An example is the preparation for the enlargement of the Union. Another example is the launch of a plan of action for employment, the so-called Amsterdam Special Action Programme (ASAP). Loans are now also being provided in labour-intensive fields such as health and education. Furthermore, financing of investments in urban renewal, environmental protection and TENs is made available and, for the first time, risk capital is provided for innovative, rapidly growing small and medium-sized companies. Since the approval of the plan of action the bank has approved 2.3 billion euro in loans in the health and education sectors and about 560 million euro in risk capital financing in innovative SMEs. The governors have agreed to reserve one billion euro from the Bank's net result in three years in order to stimulate the development of the risk capital markets in the EU member states.

The Board of Governors has approved the guidelines for a new strategic framework elaborated by the Board of Directors in connection with the new capital increase. Within this framework, the EIB will continue to direct its efforts towards peripheral economic regions of the European Union, and this fits in exactly with its main task: supporting economic convergence and integration in the European Union. The Bank will also continue to offer support in other important policy fields of the EU, such as the construction of TENs, the international competitiveness of European industry, SMEs, energy supplies, the environment and the European Union's external co-operation and development policy.'

How does the EIB regard the development of the euro capital market and what role can it play in this?

Mr. De Korte: 'From the very start we have capitalised on the development of the euro capital market and have even anticipated upon it. We have been a catalyst in that development. By means of loans from the EIB, our clients could more easily gain access to funds on other European capital markets. In the 1970s and 1980s, we already fulfilled the role of cross-border "financial engineer". Actually, we had to because we often had to swap from one currency to another one. We also considered that it was our task to cultivate the different domestic capital markets; examples like Matador, Navigator and the Marathon bond markets come to mind. We thus witnessed the birth of segments of the European euro capital market, which would become sub-markets of the euro capital market in the making.

The ECU subsequently appeared and there as well we were the first to use it as a basket currency for the denomination of bond loans. The ECU bond market's development was fostered by EIB management. By the way, the French government was rather active in this field and we co-operated a lot. We then served the euro capital market by enhancing its liquidity by means of euro tributary operations, such that bonds initially launched in national currencies became fungible. These are now "blended together". In this development the Bank as "borrower" plays an important role in the structuring of the euro capital market. It was so important to first develop the issue techniques of markets such as the Matador market, the Navigator market and the Marathon market as international Peseta, Escudo and Drachma capital markets in such a way that they were harmonious with the other markets at the international European level and thus compatible with them. Otherwise you can introduce a euro currency at a given moment, but if the techniques are not compatible and the clearing systems are not geared to one another and the bonds cannot be traded, you end up with a partitioned market. That is why it was so vitally important in the 1980s to first bring the markets in line with one another and create greater homogeneity.

This is a feature of the European Investment Bank many people are not familiar with. We are seen as a bank that lends money, but people do not always realise how important the borrowing and the structure of the borrowing operations have been. Thus the EIB not only plays an important role on the asset side, but also on the liability side. This dual role is quite clearly one of our added values.'

How does the system of liquid benchmark issues operate in practice?

Mr. De Korte: 'Since January 1999 we have been implementing a clear strategy with respect to large liquid benchmark loans. Here too, the policy is not just to leave matters as they are, but also to think about the future. Besides large liquid products there is a need for customised investment products, otherwise the market thins out. It would then mature and develop fully in one direction, but lag behind in other directions. It is thus necessary to address the particular preferences of private investors, who sometimes require, for instance, low coupons with matching low issue prices or divergent maturities that do not fit benchmark loans. The market also requires structured loans, possibly with relationships between shares and bond loans or dual currency elements.

Out of a total borrowing in 1999 of about 30 billion euro, of which we would expect about two-thirds to be denominated in euro, we think that about 40% will be devoted to euro benchmark operations and several billions to more structured euro operations (customised). The remainder will continue to be denominated mainly in US dollars, Swiss franks and British pounds. We will therefore not be restricted to one area. Because we are a borrower on the global capital markets, we are not only active in euros, even though the euro is our most important currency. We have substantial programmes in other currencies, even in South African rands, for example.'

What can the EIB do in the various sub-markets that other banks cannot do?

Mr. De Korte: 'The EIB has a different objective than a merchant bank and finances objectives like regional investments, environmental protection and employment. It must raise money for this. First of all, we have substantial capital and reserves behind us. We have a triple-A rating, which very few commercial banks have. We are, however, not able to match the borrowing rates of the German government which has also the triple-A status but is involved in even larger borrowing operations than us. Our spread is comparable to that of the Netherlands. Belgium and Portugal are rather less favourable as is the case with Italy, even though it is a large country.

There were times when the Netherlands had lower borrowing rates than Germany, but this has changed. In fact, the Netherlands now pays relatively more for the financing of its national debt than it did previously. In the past, the Dutch state was a large fish in a small pond – the pond being the Dutch guilder capital market. Now, the Dutch state is a medium-sized fish in a much larger euro capital market pond.'

In the future, shouldn't the EIB fulfil a role financing budgetary deficits? At the moment, Ministry of Finance agents take care of this financing.

Mr. De Korte: 'That is up to the agents themselves, although I do understand their problems. The agents of the medium-sized sovereign borrowers may be able to solve their problems by combining forces. This of course applies to the agents of member states with the same profile and the same rating, otherwise there will not be any point in doing this. The market has not yet fully crystallized. The EIB is allowed to raise money for productive investments but, by virtue of its statutory terms of reference, not to finance balance of payments or budgetary deficits. Thus, under its current "Statute", it cannot assume the role of funding mechanism for member states.'

Banks are merging. To what extent is it still necessary to maintain the system of primary dealers for the European Investment Bank?

Mr. De Korte: 'With all the mergers there are fewer larger players on the capital market. Nevertheless, a particular relationship with the banks is required and that must be covered by the terms of a contract. This is done by means of the "primary dealership": rights and duties with respect to the market are established by means of rules of play. The participants have the duty to maintain the market, to buy and sell at competitive prices, and to report about this, etc. It is a good idea for the group to be as large as possible so that the markets can be completely covered. However, the group must not become too large or it will be unworkable. Incidentally, our "primary dealer group" is open: after a period of time we sit around the table and promote some dealers to the position of primary dealer, while others may take their leave. We only want to work with banks that represent the markets; if not, we have to make changes.

In this respect I should refer you to our EARNs programme (Euro Area Reference Note Issuance Facility). We launch our future "euro benchmark issues" under this programme, the primary dealers being ABN-AMRO, Paribas, Deutsche Bank, HSBC Markets, Nomura International, Santander Investment, IMI (Banca d'Intermediazione Mobiliare), Goldman Sachs, Merrill Lynch International and Warburg Dillon Read. In this way we have covered the entire globe and that indicates how much we need primary dealers. In fact, they are our consuls.'

One of the tasks of the European Investment Bank is to contribute to the balanced development of the European Union. Which instruments does it use to do this?

Mr. De Korte: 'Once again, stimulation of a balanced development particularly plays a very important role in our lending operations.

"Balanced" in this respect means that the poorer regions must be more involved in the economic integration. Examples of this include the major infrastructure projects of the past in southern Italy, and the bridges and connections in Portugal and in Greece later on. There are telecommunications and transport infrastructures, such as the bridge and tunnel connections between Denmark and Sweden which are 50% financed by the EIB.

Whereas our initial task and objective was to take on the regional development in the poorer regions, these days we also concentrate very much on the improvement of European infrastructures, first and foremost transport, but also telecommunications and energy. See the

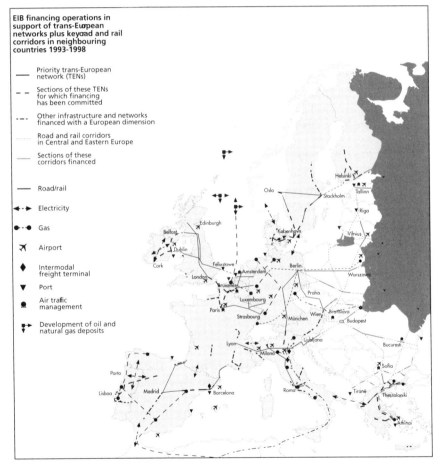

Table: Infrastructural loans from the EIB

following table with all the infrastructures in Europe for which the EIB has provided loans in the past five years.

In the eighties, a third objective was added, i.e. the protection of the environment and the quality of life (urban renewal). A fourth objective is to stimulate the competitiveness of the European business community. European companies like Mercedes Benz, Fiat, Philips, Akzo requiring corporate loans do not have to go directly to the capital market, but can also turn to us for long-term projects. This fourth objective does not only apply to large companies, but also small and medium-sized ones which we contact via mediating banks and other financial institutions, which take out credit facilities with us and subsequently lend to the small and medium-sized business sector in the form of long-term credit.

I already referred to the Amsterdam Special Action Programme (ASAP), with projects supporting growth and employment. These include the modernisation of infrastructures in the field of education and health. We stimulate the provision of venture capital towards innovative, rapidly growing small and medium-sized businesses via intermediaries.

We have been fairly successful with this: within the period of one and a half years we have developed into a major provider of venture capital.'

What has the EIB done for the Netherlands and Belgium?

Mr. De Korte: 'Just to give you a few examples in the Netherlands, quite some time ago we co-financed the flower auctions in Aalsmeer, Philips' semiconductor production and Martinair aircraft. We provided global loans to large Dutch banks like ABN-AMRO, RABO, ING, the NIB, the Bank Nederlandse Gemeenten and SNS Bank. We had DSM in our portfolio, KLM, the innovative Demkolec coal gasification plant in Buggenum, combined heat and power plants together with waste incineration ovens, air traffic control, container terminals in the Port of Rotterdam, the KPN Telecom mobile telephone network, a Stork-Wärtsila diesel production unit in Zwolle and dike reinforcement in the province of Gelderland. All in all, a fair number of projects, but still modest in comparison to what we do in other member states. That doesn't matter though. If investments in the Netherlands can be financed in another manner, either directly via the capital market or via the commercial banking system, we don't have any problem with that. We strive toward complementarity, mainly by operating where we can really provide added value.

Our lending in Belgium covers a wide spectrum of economic activity, nevertheless I would like to mention infrastructure as being a core sector over the past years. It often concerns large trans-European schemes such as high-speed rail infrastructure, for instance the section connecting Brussels with the French network and, beyond, the Channel Tunnel and the two sections Brussels-Antwerp and Brussels-Liège as part of the link between Paris-Brussels-Cologne-Amsterdam-London. We have also contributed towards financing a section of the A8 motorway, connecting Brussels with Lille and Liège, a link between the E25 and E40 motorways at Liège, and improved facilities for the European air traffic control (ATC) system at Eurocontrol, as well as the Belgian ATC. Furthermore, we have financed container terminal investment in the port of Antwerp and several environmental projects, such as waste water collection and treatment facilities in Flanders and industrial investment projects with positive environmental implications. Of course, there are many more projects to be mentioned, although I will confine myself to the natural-gas-fired power stations at Drogenbos, near Brussels, and Seraing, near Liège, trans-European gas transmission schemes, as well as telecommunications modernisation and extension. As in other EU countries, the EIB supports investment by SMEs through intermediary banks.'

The European Investment Bank is also active in non-EU countries.
Which criteria are applied in this respect?

Mr. De Korte: 'We can distinguish four groups of countries in that respect. First of all, there are the so-called Lomé countries in Africa, the Caribbean region and the Pacific Ocean. During the past five years, these countries were jointly provided with loans worth two billion euros. It looks as though the fourth Lomé protocol, which runs out in 2000, will not be continued. The operations will be performed slightly differently with a greater focus on the private sectors in those countries.

As a matter of fact, these loans are usually subsidised. The charges associated with the loan conditions that we must impose as a commercial institution – because in that sense we are a commercial institution – must be eased. The EU member states take care of this.

The second group of countries covers a large number of non-EU member states around the Mediterranean where our lending operations make a contribution to the implementation of the European-Mediterranean partnership. For example, we provide 40% or 50% finance for all gas infrastructure between Algeria and the network in the EU, via Italy and Spain. That network is then linked to other gas pipelines that enter Europe from the North Sea and from Russia, thus creating a pan-European network. In the Mediterranean region we are also concerned with the financing of projects in the environmental field. Among other things, EU subsidies are provided for EIB loans for water purification, the cleaning of the Mediterranean Sea and other environmental projects.

We then come to the area that is receiving the most interest right now: Central and Eastern Europe. There we have been assigned an extra large role because most of these countries belong to the first group of new accession countries. On account of this entry perspective, we even take on commitments there at our own risk. Other countries in Eastern Europe, such as Rumania and Bulgaria, do not belong to the first group, but we provide countries in both groups with loans subject to the same conditions. In the case of the second group, however these are not provided at our own risk but with guarantees under the so-called provisioning from the European budget. After all, the political risks of part of these investments must naturally be accommodated somehow.

Finally, we have a mandate in Latin America and Asia. The projects in question are of mutual benefit. The objective is to mainly support European companies operating under political risks. We ensure that this risk is covered and in turn make use of the provisioning of the European Union. This facility, for which there is often much more demand than we can cater for, functions well.

That is what we do in third countries, but I should emphasise that everything we do outside the Union is limited in comparison to what we do within it. About 90% of our balance sheet consists of activities within the Union and the accession countries.'

How is strategy determined by the EIB?

Mr De Korte: 'First of all, let me return to the subject of the Bank's structure, in the first place the Board of Governors, which meets once a year in Luxembourg. The people involved are the same as those who, as Ministers of Finance in the Ecofin Council, may be dealing with subjects that concern the Bank. In such a discussion about the bank in the Ecofin Council, the President of the EIB is present to provide information. Under the Board of Governors is the Board of Directors, a non-resident board that meets with us nine or ten times a year and which grants approval for the operations that we prepare in the Bank.

Under this is the executive body, the "Management Committee", consisting of eight members of which I am one. We meet every week and have a sizeable agenda with considerable consequences. We decide by means of consensus and in co-operation with senior staff. That is how the Bank is managed. The strategy is ultimately determined by the

Governors or sometimes by the government leaders. The European Council, for example, decided that the EIB should perform venture capital operations within the scope of the development of employment and growth. One billion of our reserves were released to serve as a buffer for the risk. In this case a strategy was "imposed" upon us which subsequently had to be substantiated by means of a "corporate operational plan".'

As a financial and economic factor, where does Europe stand with respect to the US and Asia?

Mr. De Korte: 'If we compare monetary depreciation and inflation in the eleven euro countries with that in the US, we see that there is absolutely no need to worry about the underlying value of the euro. This only becomes a problem if the underlying value is much stronger than the external value. The Treaty then states that the Ministers of Finance must intervene. That is not the case at the moment. Where the long-term value of the euro is concerned, I say nothing new when I maintain that the underlying value of the euro in the long term is such – even if you look at the current account of the balance of payments – that we do not have to worry about it. The dollar is the currency of a country which has had a balance of payments deficit for the past eighteen years already. The European Union, in this case the eleven euro countries, has had a balance of payments surplus for years. Therefore, the time must come in the medium term when the euro has a strong underlying stable value.

There was once a Belgian professor who dared to predict in the nineteen fifties that the dollar would be unpegged from the gold standard (Bretton Woods). No one believed him at the time and it took twelve years before he was proved correct. It was very easy, the world was flooded with dollars so that the parity with the gold standard could no longer be maintained at a given moment. We have now been faced with a glut of dollars for the past nineteen years. The world still has confidence in the US economy and in the way in which Americans deal with all those funds. So there is still nothing wrong. Will it stay that way? Things can change, that's what history has taught us.'

How do you regard 'IT-driven finance'?

Mr. De Korte: 'IT provides us with avelanches of information with which we must do something. You have to make selections and make the information accessible.

You can regard IT as the possibility for an organisation to internally document its business activities. We strive to set up the Bank's business management in such a way in the field of communication technology, by means of data warehousing and data mining, that a transaction only has to be entered once and subsequently handled upstream and downstream: thus enriching, supplementing, updating and checking. In this way we attempt to create a single integrated database instead of a separate databank for the borrowing activities, a separate database for the lending activities, a separate database for accountancy, etc. There in particular we see the great value of the IT evolution. We consider IT-driven finance to be extremely important and it is therefore taken very seriously. At the moment, we are determining our strategy for the first few years of the 21st century. We have the feeling – where our technological infrastructure and our applications are concerned – that we should actually have more than is strictly necessary at the moment. We consider that the operation should not only produce cost savings, but should also be of assistance for the creation of more added value.'

One of the special areas of attention of the EIB is the infrastructure. How does the bank proceed with the assessment of these risks?

Mr. De Korte: 'Three-quarters of our funding relates to infrastructure. The underlying projects are sometimes extremely complex and there are many aspects involved, such as public/private partnerships (PPPs). We are familiar with all forms of co-operation in this field. In the European Union, we are involved in several PPPs, all of which have different means of finance. In this respect, we act as an intermediary for experience to Central and Eastern Europe. For instance, we hold detailed discussions with various national governments there and they listen because they know that we speak on the basis of considerable experience.'

A few figures as at 31 December 1998

– Subscribed capital: 100 billion euros, of which the Netherlands accounts for 4.0%
– Maximum gearing ratio is 250%
– Balance sheet total: 176 billion euros
– Outstanding and committed credits: 155 billion euros
– Aggregate amount of borrowings: 124 billion euros

In 1998:

– 29 billion euros were extended in credits
– the gross capital market borrowing was 30 billion euros
– 22 currencies (before swaps) were used

– The expected capital market borrowing in 1999 is about 30 billion euros

---

9. Increasing liberalisation of financial markets has implications for national policymaking

In conversation with the Dutch Minister of Finance, Mr. G. Zalm

More than ever before, strategic finance is a hot topic in the public sector. Not only are there many important aspects in this sector itself, including the globalisation of the financial markets, the role of investment banks in the financial and economic world and, last but not least, corporate governance and government governance, but the public sector (particularly regulatory and supervisory government bodies) also has the opportunity to regulate, or at least to steer strategic financial flows in the private sectors.

Mr. G. Zalm

In the Netherlands, a key player in this respect is of course the Dutch Minister of Finance, Mr. Gerrit Zalm. What are his opinions about the hot issues in Strategic Finance and where is intervention required in his opinion? A probing interview with him on the subject.

The influence of shareholder value is increasing. What do you think of this development? Should Dutch corporations protect themselves for this?

Mr. Zalm: 'First of all, I would like to note that the concept of shareholder value can easily give rise to misunderstandings. People sometimes think that creating shareholder value is automatically to the detriment of other stakeholders (such as employees). This is not true. Both shareholders and employees share the same interest, which is a well-performing corporation. In my view, attention for shareholder value therefore does not mean that management is only focused on creating value for shareholders. It does imply that management is accountable for its policy to the shareholders.

The concept of shareholder value originates from the US, where management places quite considerable emphasis on communicating with its shareholders. Another concept that was developed in this field in the US is investor relations. Both shareholder value and investor relations form part of the broader concept of corporate governance. Furthermore, being accountable in the US means more than just communicating with the shareholders. Unsatisfied shareholders speak out at general meetings, or "vote with their feet", i.e. by selling in the market they cause a devaluation of the share price. A lower share price may harm the reputation of the management, imply lower value for existing stock compensation plans, and increase the possibility of a hostile takeover. Because of this, both the direct and indirect influence of shareholders will have a disciplining effect on management.

In the Netherlands, attention is increasingly being paid to corporate governance and the role of the shareholders. Partly due to increased private and institutional shareholdings, shareholders are starting to raise their voices more often. Given the market discipline of shareholder influence that I just mentioned, I think this development should be welcomed. Most management teams now actually take the voice of shareholders seriously. However, due to various anti-takeover devices, shareholders cannot always genuinely cast their vote at meetings, and a hostile takeover still has a low probability of success. Don't get me wrong; some protection can be useful, because it is undesirable to allow shareholders to wrest control from the management at any particular moment in time. But in my view, anti-takeover devices should not be misused to shield management from accountability. In this context, it is worth mentioning that a law is pending in the Dutch Parliament that gives shareholders, if certain criteria are met, the right to challenge anti-takeover devices in court.'

How does the work of the Peters Committee relate to the corporate governance discussion?

Mr. Zalm: 'In June 1997, the Peters Committee formulated forty recommendations in order to improve the corporate governance of Dutch corporations. The recommendations apply to "peacetime situations", that is to say, they were not meant to apply in takeover situations. Subsequently, a Monitoring Committee (known as "Peters II") has examined the extent to which corporations complied with the forty recommendations during the year 1997. The results of the Monitoring

Committee, which were reported in December 1998, showed that most corporations had applied many of the recommendations pertaining to the structure and the working method of the board. Moreover, recent research indicates that Dutch boards, due to the two-tier structure with a separation between top-management and board of directors, for the most part perform above the European average. Due to the Peters Committee, corporate governance has found its way onto the agendas of listed companies, which is a notable achievement. However, and this is a repetition of my answer to the preceding question, the report of the Monitoring Committee also showed little progress on the recommen-dations that were supposed to improve the influence of shareholders. Some argue that shareholders are not interested in more influence, thereby pointing at the fairly large level of absenteeism at general meet-ings. However, this appears to be a chicken-and-egg problem; one could also argue that shareholders do not attend meetings because they have no influence due to various anti takeover devices. Moreover, some institutional investors with shares in many Dutch companies find it fairly expensive and time-consuming to attend all meetings. This problem is even more relevant for foreign (institutional) investors. It is in this light that one should see the legislative initiatives to facilitate proxy voting and to reduce the effect of anti-takeover devices in peacetime situations that the government announced in a letter to Parliament in May 1999. Implementing these initiatives would imply that shareholders have more means of casting their vote at the general meeting. It is then up to the shareholders to use their increased possibilities.'

The supervisory structure in particular seems to capture your attention. There are currently three relevant authorities for financial services, i.e. the Dutch Central Bank (Banking Supervisor), the Verzekeringskamer (Insurance Supervisor) and the Stichting Toezicht Effectenverkeer (Securities Supervisor). These supervisory bodies co-operate through the Board of Financial Supervisors (RFT). Why has this structure been chosen instead of a single supervisory authority?

Mr. Zalm: 'The emergence of financial conglomerates and the ongoing development of hybrid financial products point to the need for a cross-sector perspective. There are several ways in which this may be achieved. The first option would be to restructure supervision by objective, similar to recent reforms in Australia and the UK. The second scenario would be to supplement the sectoral model with a cross-sector element.

The successful track record of the sectoral model in the Netherlands has led to a preference for the second, more gradual approach. I have therefore chosen to establish a Board of Financial Supervisors in which the three financial supervisory bodies participate. A desirable feature of this model is that problems of transition may be avoided. In addition, we avoid the discussion concerning the role of the monetary authority vis-à-vis prudential supervision, which in other countries has led to a separation of the two functions. The model chosen does justice to the strengths of the sectoral model, while introducing the flexibility that may be needed if market forces should require further adaptations to the structure of supervision in the future.

It may be interesting to note that a need for a cross-sector platform is felt at the European level too. The European Commission has therefore established the Financial Services Policy Group; our Board of Financial Supervisors will be compatible with this Group.'

It appears that the Dutch Competition Authority and the Dutch Central Bank both deal with the banking sector (consider, for example, the intended merger between Rabobank and Achmea). Was it really the intention that the competence of the Dutch Competition Authority should reach that far?

Mr. Zalm: 'Since January 1998 the Dutch Business Competition Act has been in force. This legislation states that the Dutch Competition Authority (Nederlandse Mededingingsautoriteit, NMa) will be responsible for the supervision of the competition aspects of concentrations. However, during a two-year transitional period, the financial supervisors will conduct supervision on concentrations in the financial sector, as before. Only from 1 January 2000, will the NMa bear full responsibility for the supervision of competition in the financial sector. Simultaneously however, financial supervisors will continue to review the effects of concentrations, other than those related to competition, including the effects on financial stability and consumer protection. A potential outcome of this separation is that the financial supervisors and the NMa disagree in their verdict concerning particular concentrations. An exemplary case is when an intended concentration will prevent a bankruptcy that threatens the stability of the financial system. To deal with such "emergency situations" a special procedure will be created that should lead to a decision in each case. The precise formulation of this procedure is left to the supervisors and the NMa, and is currently in preparation. I expect that a conclusion will soon be reached in the matter.'

The risk of derivatives is increasing; do you plan policy responses to this development?

Mr. Zalm: 'Your question refers to the risk derived from the use of derivatives, but I would also like to stress that derivatives are mostly used for the mitigation of risk. For example, banks generally use options and futures as a way of hedging exchange risk and interest rate risk, just like firms do. Although hedging reduces risk by definition, the use of derivatives may lead to new risks in some cases. For example, counterparties of over-the-counter (OTC) derivatives (the OTC market is characterised by bilateral transactions between counterparties) may suddenly fail to live up to their obligations resulting from adverse market movements, thus introducing credit risk. Furthermore, derivatives are conditional claims, and may contain a legal risk if their enforceability is uncertain because of ill-defined conditions.

Policymakers and supervisors recognise both aspects of derivatives. On the one hand, proposals are made within the EU and the Basle framework to reward the use of derivatives by providing capital relief should a risk be reduced through the use of derivatives. On the other hand, given the potential dangers I just mentioned, special attention is given to the inherent risk in such derivative products. These aspects are recognised in the preparation of EU legislation on this matter.'

How would you regard a truly cross-border merger between a Dutch and a foreign financial institution?

Mr. Zalm: 'The first thing is to understand that the necessary approval of the authorities does not alter the fact that financial institutions are in principle free to choose their own domicile. More generally, consolidation processes are international economic developments. Nevertheless, we have to make sure that adequate supervision of such cross-border financial institutions remains possible. Therefore, Dutch supervisors use several criteria to judge a merger of a Dutch Bank with a foreign institution. Examples of these criteria are that the organisational structure of the new institution is transparent, and that effective supervision can be maintained. Other perspectives from which the merger will be judged are the potential effects on the market structure and the level of competition. In this respect it is important to note that from 1 January 2000, mergers within the Dutch banking system will be judged by the NMa.'

What is the influence of the euro on the functioning of the European capital market?

Mr. Zalm: 'By eliminating currency risk within the euro area, the adoption of the euro offers the opportunity to end the segmentation of national markets and transform them into a deep and liquid capital market. The euro, however, is not the only factor influencing the integration of capital markets within the euro area. Further work needs to be done on eliminating differences in tax and regulatory regimes and on aligning business practices. Therefore, work is underway on the basis of an EU action plan for the completion of the single market in financial services.'

How do you view the exchange rate development of the euro?

Mr. Zalm: 'I do not comment on actual developments in the euro exchange rate. However, in general, it is useful to distinguish between the internal and the external value of the euro. The objective of monetary policy by the European Central Bank is to maintain the internal value of the euro, which is price stability. There is no exchange rate target, but price stability means that in the long run the euro will be a strong currency. This does not mean that exchange rate developments will be neglected. The ECB will have to judge what influence exchange rate developments have on inflation in the euro area, since exchange rate developments influence import prices.'

Where should Europe go as financial power in relation to the US and Asia? Which changes in relative strength do you expect in the future, and will these powers persist?

Mr. Zalm: 'The central question is not that of power, but of responsibility. The euro is one of the key international currencies, and this brings with it a special responsibility for the functioning of the international monetary system. Consequently representation in organisations that discuss topics relating to the international monetary system is now more equal than it was previously. For example, in the G-7, the President of the European Central Bank and the President of the Euro-11 group now take part when issues are discussed that are of particular relevance to EMU.'

What do you think of the creation of a single European stock exchange, and what will be the pace of integration? Will national exchanges remain to exist for the small caps?

Mr. Zalm: 'The idea of a European stock exchange is of course a logical one. Financial markets, as well as the investors on those markets, are becoming more and more internationally oriented. The introduction of the euro gives a further impetus to integration. A first step towards a single European exchange has been taken by the signing of a letter of intent by eight European stock exchanges. Recently, these exchanges have decided to create an electronic trading platform on which 300 large European stocks will be listed.

The pace of integration mainly depends on two factors. First, harmonisation on a number of issues is needed; this can range from trading systems and opening hours to tax regimes. Secondly, possible competition from other parties can be an important impetus for rapid integration. Here I do not only refer to competition from other countries, but also to the development of fully automated trading systems. As I just mentioned, only the larger European stocks will be traded on the single European stock exchange, because international investors are sufficiently informed about these stocks. I expect that the national exchanges will not only continue to play an important role in the trading of the smaller stocks, but also in the introduction of new stocks. This is important, because the creation of a "European Champions League" should not prevent smaller firms from having access to the capital market.'

In view of the globalisation of the financial markets, is it still possible for a Minister of Finance to pursue a particular policy, or does he have to passively observe how this is dictated by the financial markets and cross-border conglomeration of financial institutions and other multinational businesses?

Mr. Zalm: 'It is no secret that increasing liberalisation of financial markets has implications for national policymaking. Market participants will partly base their decisions on comparisons of different regulatory regimes. However, it would be wrong to conclude that a country should lower regulation to an absolute minimum, in order to prevent a massive exodus from businesses and employees. New developments always have the potential to cause externalities that lead to a suboptimal outcome for all market participants. Examples of such externalities can be found in systemic risk or financial fraud.

I believe that policies which are both directed to the elimination of externalities and responsive to new developments will be welcomed by the marketplace.'

10. Behave properly: that's the way to guarantee return

In conversation with Professor S. Benartzi

More and more research is being conducted to find out how individual behaviour influences decisions, particularly those in the financial field. This influence can be exerted with respect to financial decisions at various levels and ranging from strategic to operational decisions. Where the typical private individual is concerned, an important financial decision is obviously how he invests his funds. In this connection, we can for instance think of the system whereby people must invest during their active working years for when they are pensioned or take early retirement.

Prof. S. Benartzi

An eminent researcher, who has examined the influence of behaviour on individual financial decisionmaking, is Professor Shlomo Benartzi from UCLA (1968). He has conducted research in this field, which is generally referred to by the term 'behavioural finance'. We asked him how the research was developing, what his findings are and what still has to be covered in this field in the future.

The central element in your research is referred to as 'equity premium'. Could you please explain the term in a little more detail? What is the practical importance of this concept?

Benartzi: 'The equity premium is simply the difference between the returns on an index of stocks and a safe investment such as short-term government securities. This is one of the fundamental issues in finance because it relates to where you invest your money and the balance between risky and riskless securities. This is basically the subject that Richard Thaler and I covered in our paper "Myopic Loss Aversion and the Equity Premium Puzzle". The equity premium puzzle refers to the empirical fact that stocks have outperformed bonds over the last century by a surprisingly large margin.'

In relation to this you introduced the behavioural concept of 'loss aversion'. Could you explain this?

Prof. Benartzi: 'Loss aversion refers to the tendency for individuals to be more sensitive to reductions in their levels of well being than to increases. Of course, in a model with loss aversion, the more often an investor evaluates his portfolio, or the shorter his horizon, the less attractive he will find a high mean, high risk investment such as stocks. It is assumed that investors are "loss averse", meaning that they are distinctly more sensitive to losses than to gains, and that they evaluate their portfolios frequently.

Empirical estimates of loss aversion are typically in the neighbourhood of 2, meaning the disutility of giving something up is twice as great as the utility of receiving it.'

In the long term you speak about 'myopic loss aversion'. Please could you explain exactly what this term means?

Prof. Benartzi: ' Two factors contribute to an investor being unwilling to bear the risks associated with holding equities, loss aversion and a short evaluation period. We referred to this combination "myopic loss aversion". When decision makers are loss averse, they will become more willing to take risks if they evaluate their performance infrequently. Suppose an investor must choose between a risky asset that pays an expected 7 percent per year with a standard deviation of 20 percent (like stocks) and a safe asset with pays a sure 1 percent. Obviously, the attractiveness of the risky asset will depend on the time horizon of the investor.

So there are two components. One component is loss aversion, which refers to the fact that people think illogically about losses, so the pain of suffering a loss is about twice that of the enjoyment and pleasure of having an equivalent gain. The other is the myopic component. Because people tend to count their money very often they tend to be myopic, i.e. they focus on short-term gains and losses, rather than taking a long-term perspective. If you think about the daily stock return, the likelihood of stocks outperforming bonds is about 50/50 on a given day. People who count their money often and focus on short-term losses would avoid stocks. So this is how myopic loss aversion relates to the equity premium. We find that the "typical" investor has a horizon of about one year. We feel that if people count their money less often they would put more money into equities and the equity premium would probably be lower. The question is how we can stop people from focusing on short-term losses.

To do this we conducted a few experiments. In one of them we presented people with an annual return on a stock fund and a bond fund and asked them to decide how much to put in each fund. In this case they put about 40% in stocks. In another version we showed employees what the returns would look like over a 30-year horizon. They put 90% in stocks, because we basically made them stop thinking about short-term losses. Based on the way in which the risk and return profile of and investment is presented, we were able to have people go from one extreme of investing conservatively to the other extreme of investing fairly aggressively. This is how we were able to mitigate, or at least minimise the effect of myopic loss aversion. We are not saying that people should be 100% in stock, but we do say that people shouldn't count their money too often. If you are a long-term investor you should only think of the long-term outcome of your investment policy and not be distracted by the short term.'

Do you think that the fund managers are already using the results of your studies?

Prof. Benartzi: 'There are a few investment consulting firms in the US, such as Financial Engines and Iberton Associates, which provide advice on how to invest money. In providing they advice they focus on the long-term result or the retirement income rather than on short-term market fluctuation. They focus on what the retirement income would be by investing in different funds, and that way they try to mitigate the short-term or myopic focus on short-term losses. Where pension funds are concerned, it is rather puzzling why they do not invest a higher proportion in stocks, given the historical equity premium and the fact that pension funds essentially have an infinite time horizon. Myopic loss aversion appears to offer an explanation for this. While the pension fund is likely to exist for many years, the pension fund manager does not expect to be in the same job forever. He will have to make regular reports on the funding level of the pension plan and the returns on funds assets. This short horizon creates a conflict of interest between the pension fund manager and the beneficiaries.'

There is a world-wide trend towards defined contribution saving plans and growing interest in privatised social security plans. Can you explain these systems?

Prof. Benartzi: 'There is a trend towards letting individuals have some control, some investment autonomy, over the investment in their retirement portfolio. Depending upon the return on their portfolio they would have more or less money on retirement. In another study Thaler and I found that people tend to spread their money evenly among the investment choices. For example, if you offer people a stock fund and a bond fund they spread the money fifty-fifty between them. Depending on the menu of choices being offered, individuals become more or less conservative. On the one hand, people might take too much risk and then the government would have to bail them out of poverty at retirement. On the other hand, they would take too little risk and their funds would not grow fast enough to provide sufficient long-term fundings. In my opinion, most people are not aware of what diversification means. An example of this is that they do not invest much internationally, they prefer the domestic market. In my research I have shown that many investors have very naïve notions about diversification. Evidence suggests that some people spread their contributions evenly across the investment options irrespective of the particular mix of options in a plan. One of the implications of this is that the array of funds offered to plan participants can have a strong influence on the asset allocation people select; as the number of stock funds increases, so does the allocation to equities. The empirical evidence confirms that the array of funds being offered affects the resulting asset allocation.

The results of my research highlight difficult issues regarding the design of retirement saving plans, both public and private. The question that arises is what is the right mix of fixed income and equity funds. If the plan offers many fixed-income funds the participants might invest too conservatively. Similarly, if the plan offers many equity funds the employees might invest too aggressively.'

What are possible future research topics and what is the expected evolution in behavioural finance?

Prof. Benartzi: 'I hope that behavioural finance will focus more on individual decision making. How individuals make their financial decisions. Part of this would concern major decisions like buying a house, saving for retirement, but unfortunately most of the research in finance at the moment is about prices and how we price different assets. This is not everything, we also have to understand how individuals make decisions. Even if the price in the market is unaffected by their mistakes, it is still interesting to see how individuals make investment decisions and help them to make better investment and other financial decisions. Therefore, I think that the next step is not just looking at prices, but looking at individual decision making. Behavioural science has a lot to teach us, it can help us to understand how people make decisions and how we can help them to do so.'

Do you think behavioural science should be covered within the Faculty of Psychology or the Faculty of Economics?
Prof. Benartzi: 'I think it will be disastrous if it's only included in just one of the two. We should adopt an interdisciplinary approach. if we classify something as psychology or economics then we already limit our ability to dwell on many different areas in order to understand the phenomena that we are studying.'

From the interview with Professor Benartzi it is clear that private individuals do indeed take decisions which cannot be described as purely rational, but rather are imbued with their behaviour and particularly by elements such as those which are termed "myopic loss aversion" by Professor Benartzi. The major question to be asked is whether professionals, when they are familiar with this behaviour, are able to use the information to develop investment funds and other systems that capitalise on this wise or unwise behaviour and as a result try to convert it into extra profit for the fund manager.'

11. Supervision and management. On people's sense of responsibility, cruel markets and presentation

In conversation with Professor J.R. Glasz

Perhaps the most important objective of a company is to maximise its shareholder value, a concept that has been the focus for some years now in discussions about corporate governance and the relationship between corporate governance and internal management and internal control. It ultimately has to do with organisational aspects and the aspect of supervision. Within Dutch companies, the supervisory function is performed by supervisory boards. Someone with experience in supervisory boards is former deputy judge, former senator, former Dean of the National Bar and

Prof. J.R. Glasz

currently practising lawyer and professor of Corporate Governance at the University of Amsterdam, Prof. Jaap Glasz (1935).

Prof. Glasz: 'I was a supervisory director for companies quite early on. At the age of 26 I received my first seat on a supervisory board in my father's family business. I now have seats on various supervisory boards where I oversee a wide range of business. At Fortis I work in great abstraction with ratios, not operationally like I used to do at the savings bank where we kept an eye on exposures each month. My seat at Coca-Cola is even more operational in nature. There I've been learning about crisis management in this day and age and about how a subsidiary of a US company works. In the US, they go about their work differently than we do here. I am also a supervisory director for a subsidiary of Glaxo, a company in the UK. They have their own particular work ethic there as well. And the French have their own style, too. That's been my experience as supervisory director at Citroën Nederland and – in France – at Bongrain. According to French standards, Bongrain is quite avant-garde, since France has a single-tier board system. In this case, they had taken advantage of the legal possibilities to establish a conseil de sur-véillance. I share the board with an Argentine, a German and a Spaniard.

There I acquire plenty of material for my lectures in Corporate Governance at the University of Amsterdam. That is an optional subject in the second, third and fourth years of study.'

How would you define yourself as a corporate governance lawyer?

Prof. Glasz: 'It would be more productive to stick to a working defi-nition than to give an exhaustive description. Corporate governance literally means something like "guiding an organisation". In my eyes, corporate governance stands for giving proper direction to legal entities, such as institutions. For me, that goes further than listed com-panies alone. The law translates it as the principle of "proper admin-istration and supervision" and that, in my opinion, applies to all legal entities, for governmental bodies and such.'

What vision do you give in your lectures?

Prof. Glasz: 'I give real-life examples of organisations that have encountered problems owing to the lack of corporate governance and whose problems have something to teach us. At the same time, how-ever, I give just as many examples of organisations that have done well or are doing well today. After all, they too have something to teach us. I try to highlight the problem areas. At this stage of their studies, I assume that the students already understand the theory. In my first lecture, I ask those present to read the newspapers carefully for items on corporate governance. As soon as I begin the next lecture, I ask for the case of the week. That coaxes students to sharpen their focus on the newspapers, because there is always news in this area. Take for instance the question of whether an employee foundation can be used to finance its own foundations where preference shares are held. If the employee foundation is used for defensive purposes and not as a place of safekeeping for the staff's shares, does that constitute improper use? The Enterprise Section of the Amsterdam Court of Appeal handed down a decision at the same time, so we immediately incorporated it into the lecture.

The week thereafter we were presented with yet another case: may someone who is director of bank A also serve on the supervisory board of an investment bank? How should such an officer go about handling the confidential information that he becomes aware of at the invest-ment bank and that he would be required to funnel to bank A in the interest of his actual employer? The danger of a conflict of interests is enormous. Cry as we might that we do not want "American conditions", we've been importing them all along. Corporate governance has always played a role. The only difference is that now it's in the spotlight.'

Is corporate governance a question of ethics?

Prof. Glasz: 'Not just that. The criterion in the Netherlands is "proper". But what does that mean... The law does not tell us much more than that organisations need to be properly administered and supervised. This standard of proper behaviour – and that's what we call the corporate standard – ultimately comes down to its interpretation in practice. Each field of operations has its own idea on what it means. Managers, auditors, controllers and lawyers are thereby tasked with documenting these interpretations. In this way, this doctrine can be further developed. We're not talking about legal standards but rather standards that have developed in the actual business or corporate world. And yes, they have an ethical side.'

Are the forty recommendations made by the Peters commission simply a passing trend? Much ado about nothing? Or has a fundamental change taken place in business?

Prof. Glasz: 'Corporate governance is a title for making structures and rules for those principles that we have been using all along, but that have now received extra emphasis. A face-lift for corporate governance can be useful now and then. The Dutch are very receptive to influences from abroad, particularly from the UK and US. If a certain Sir Adrian Cadbury once again reformulates and sharpens this set of principles, we lose no time in closely comparing it with our own version.

I do believe that Peters has had an effect, but not so much as concerns rules for supervisory directors. Although the first twenty of the forty recommendations mainly concern supervisory directors, we had already seen these in a different form before. I myself tried to formulate a set of rules of conduct in 1989 and I recognise a lot of my ideas in many of the recommendations made by the Peters commission. Jaap Peters told me as well that they were grateful to be able to make use of my work.

When I came with the first print of the rules of conduct as I saw them, they were not exactly received with great acclaim by everyone. The incumbent generation of supervisory directors found them some-what exaggerated. They themselves were perfectly capable of deciding how a supervisory director should function. With their experience, common sense and wisdom, they did not need any trifling book from Glasz. Now we've seen an about-face in their thinking. Today's supervisory director considers it perfectly normal that he should use a checklist and that people should be able to tell him what else he should know. I believe that the threat of liability has also played a role in this respect. Take for instance the OGEM affair and Tilburgse Hypotheekbank, where people saw how serious the situation had become.

The Cadbury commission came about in the UK in the same way – as a response to major financial ruin. People started complaining at that time, and the public didn't accept it and started wondering exactly what those supervisors, those non-executives, did after all. Thereafter, we received the report from the Peters commission with its recommendations. Its effect was much greater than even the commission itself had probably hoped. Listed companies started presenting themselves much more clearly in their annual reports.

The discussion on the interest of one's own company is now a live topic again. There I see how various stakeholders might ultimately get their chance. This is because in the Netherlands, as soon as corporate governance is mentioned, people immediately jump to the conclusion that it has to do with giving shareholders more power. But that is not the whole truth. In Belgium, for example, corporate governance is seen as a means of loosening up those ties with the shareholders that have become too tight, with a view to giving more power to the company's management and supervision. In the US and the UK, corporate governance is not used to increase the power of shareholders, as their power is already dominant. There, the emphasis is placed on extra strong supervision, to create a good balance for the incumbent managers vis-à-vis their shareholders. As you see, each culture has its own emphasis. The recommendations from the Peters commission must not be misused. Corporate governance must never be allowed to become a political topic; it must remain pure, just like the objective that it hopes to achieve.'

Which is preferable? The Dutch system with its strict division between the board of supervisory directors and the board of management? Or should we switch to an Anglo-American board system where executives and non-executives make decisions as a joint body?

Prof. Glasz: 'In the Netherlands, the task of the supervisory director is twofold. His job is to supervise and to give advice. This implies that he must win the respect of the board of directors as a fully-fledged sparring partner for the managing directors. I am a proponent of technical supervision. I see it now in the share option committee where we worked together with the Confederation of Netherlands Industry and Employers (the Dutch VNO-NCW) on behalf of the Dutch Centre for Managing and Supervisory Directors (the Dutch NCD) to make recommendations and develop them with respect to formulating share options for managing directors. The question is whether the supervisors understand what they're talking about if the company's management comes with a share option scheme for managing directors. Are they familiar with the mechanism, the technique? Are they aware that they can also issue conditional share options? Do they understand the tax implications? Do they know when taxation takes place and that there is a range of tax variants from which to choose? Do they see the possibilities for attaching the allotment of share options to conditions of such a nature that performance also plays a role in the extent to which the managing director can subsequently exercise the option and keep the proceeds?

The supervisory director requires that sort of expertise and he needs to be independent. He needs to be able to give a retort to the management of the company that announces share option plans. The company might also find that the share options need to be in line with the market, since the organisation will be operating internationally. And in the US, people are familiar with remuneration proportions of 1/3 fixed salary, 1/3 annual incentives and 1/3 long-term incentives, while a managing director in the Netherlands receives a base salary of 60%, a 30% bonus and 10% options. So what then? A supervisory director then needs to know if, and to what extent, a comparison with the market is relevant. He must serve as a counterbalance, which is only possible if he is well enough informed about the mechanisms and effects of share options.'

But can supervision and management go together?

Prof. Glasz: 'Germany, the Netherlands and possibly Denmark are the only countries with a two-tier system. We can rest assured that the UK will never abandon its single-tier board system. I have incidentally seen that the French have introduced the option of a two-tier board-system, but that it is rarely used. The Dutch government recently announced in a letter that in its vision, no one should expect a major rapprochement within the European context, unless the market itself succeeds in getting the systems to converge.

At the Dutch-Belgian Fortis, where we non-executives form a single Board of Directors with the executives, I perceive little difference in the consultative structure. In my opinion, a one-tier system is also a good option, as long as the board does not get too big. If too many captains are aboard the ship, it won't work. Fortis, for example, has 24 people on its board. A few of them serve as speakers, the others are not very active. That's the way it has to be, otherwise the whole thing won't work. As a result, people seek refuge in all sorts of committees that prepare resolutions. This has made the board much more of a formalising institution. That's not the idea either, in my opinion. A separate supervisory board therefore certainly has its advantages. It's somewhat better at preserving independence than when supervisory and managing directors always form a single board together. I actually believe that the supervisory officers in both models should have the same responsibilities. That's because it still remains unclear to me to what extent the responsibility of the non-executive director is supposed to be greater than that of the supervisory director. I my opinion, this must have an impact on their independence.

Supervision is not the same as management. Management from a distance is one of the most confusing concepts that I can imagine. That's something one sees in foundations and associations. If things go amiss, the officers sooner put the blame on someone else than accepting it themselves. That's just not right. The foundation's officers are officially responsible. The same applies to ministers. They need to make sure that they have things under control and that their department functions. That implies a efficient staff and expert, senior officials. It's the same in the world of business. The management board of a large company needs to confer very carefully with the directors of its subsidiaries and its managers. They often have a management committee. At the point that such an underpin eventually starts to crumble, the company's management cannot simply say that it is not responsible. As soon as people start avoiding their responsibilities, the system collapses.'

There is naturally a collective sense of responsibility in a one-tier system. But if a non-executive director stops by once a month, while the day-to-day management meets every Monday morning, that has to give rise to an enormous difference in positions of information?

Prof. Glasz: 'A one-tier system also needs to have different levels of liability. Anything else would be nearly impossible. This needs to be revised in Dutch company law too. The reason is that unlike in a two-tier system, there is generally no distinction between management and supervision in the same board. Under the current law, a non-executive (the de facto supervisory director) within a single-structure board of directors still receives the responsibilities of an executive. Unless he is able to exculpate himself, because he does not have the information that an executive has, for instance.'

As Chairman of the Supervisory Board of Fortis, you must ask yourself now and then what you would need to do to exercise enough control?

Prof. Glasz: 'Yes, that's true. In a small company, that's somewhat easier than in a large one. That means putting together supervisory tools, ratios, figures, key figures. Naturally, one first needs to make sure that the figures are reliable. Assuming that they are, and that one receives them in complete shape and on time, then the task of the management board is in fact not any different from that of the supervisory board. The management supervises too, since it's supposed to keep everything under control. After all, it happens to be that the members of the board of directors are supervisory directors at the operating companies. They have portfolios and have to maintain supervision. Holding company directors are essentially compliance officers at lower operational levels.

The supervisory tools should come from the reports. They need to be quick and timely and need to enable the people who use them to form a picture of the company. At Coca-Cola the supervisory directors meet once a quarter – solely to watch computer screens and presentations. Figures also provide an understanding of quality management, complaints management, logistics and repairs. That is all very advanced. But figures alone do not tell us enough. An explanation is always necessary. The exchange of ideas in particular is very important; and that's not something that can really be fed into a computer. But it is true, the larger a holding company becomes, the more you reach a higher level of abstraction down the road.'

It is often said that the true value of a company differs too much from its value as perceived on the stock exchange: this is apparently a transparency problem. Isn't the core of corporate governance to keep companies from issuing such biased information? And to keep share options from being exercised with too much gain?

Prof. Glasz: 'That is indeed a big problem because it is always difficult to trade without inside knowledge. And directors naturally always have inside knowledge. That applies to both the shares they hold and their options. In the case of share options, the director can actually choose the moment that he exercises them, thereby using his inside knowledge. However, there still has to be a way to come up with appropriate measures for this situation. One possibility might be to agree on a longer period. The best solution would be for this exercise period to end at the age for pension entitlement. After all, the reasons behind share options are as follows. Firstly, they keep people with expertise within the company. Secondly, they act as incentives for people to do their best. That's where it works both ways, since it incidentally also makes the shareholders more important. I believe that one can certainly say that the shareholder is the most important stakeholder; not the only one, but certainly the most important. The best thing is therefore to give the director the sense of being a shareholder.

As long as the supervisory directors have a good understanding of what sort of impact share options have, so that they can focus their eyes even more on the correct functioning of the share options scheme, they will do a good job. But that means that they still need to be given the chance. The task of the supervisory officer is to determine what to include in the emoluments package. The Association of Securities Holders, the Dutch VEB, wants to give this task to the shareholders and that argument will win increasing ground the more that supervisory directors are unable to fulfil the demands of their supervisory functions.

Another stakeholder is the employee component. The chairman of a trade union recently spoke of a "kleptocracy" in this context. That is naturally demagoguery. What exactly is being stolen? What harm is exercising a share option going to do to anyone? How much do share options really cost a company? Nevertheless, the reaction is under-standable: if the Unions demand moderation, it is the job of the senior management to set an example.

Another important stakeholder is politics, which has a lot to say about share option schemes. But as long as politicians keep dropping a lot of their own administrative clangers, I am inclined to believe that they would be wise to change their tune in this respect.'

Do you want supervisory directors to be better trained?

Prof. Glasz: 'Certainly, in my book on the Rules of Conduct I also posit that supervisory directorship is becoming a profession. In the past that was different. At that time the supervisory director was someone from a good family and with whom the company could make an impression. That type of person had a network, which was very nice. Now that is no longer enough. Society expects a supervisory director to truly maintain supervision. This means that the supervisory director will have to become competent. And in my eyes that's really happen-ing. Slowly but surely, the quality of the supervisory officers at major companies in the Netherlands, the two-tier board companies, is becoming quite high. The only area where people can still differ in their opinions is – certainly given the discussion on share options – whether supervisory directors are independent enough.

The ideal supervisory director is a director who has just retired from a major company and who has bade farewell to the past. In my opinion, the ideal supervisory director is someone who has his own management experience and who at the very most can jeopardise his independence by becoming a supervisory director for competitor companies. That's something that we do not like. This can pose problems with conflicting interests, particularly in the case of acquisitions and similar situations. Let's say that mister X is supervisory director at company A. This company is going to acquire company B, where mister X happens to sit on the supervisory board. It is then wise for X to keep out of the discussion. It's true that people often use the argument that X can actually be very valuable, since he is familiar with both A and B from the inside; but that is the wrong argument. A company's management can immediately feel when a supervisory director has taken a privileged position. Certain items are suddenly not put on the agenda and people start ringing up other supervisory directors, but not X. That leads to isolation and bad relations. Supervision on the other supervisory officers therefore means that one supervisory officer remains outside the situation illustrated above. The ideal supervisory officer is therefore someone who is no longer active in the area where conflicting interests are lying in wait.'

Isn't too much importance placed on shareholder value?

Prof. Glasz: 'Yes, that happens. When two candidates step forward to take over a company with the one being prepared to pay more than the other, one could naturally innocently conjecture that the former is "therefore" the better party, since the shareholder would have more to gain. But it is also very possible that such a party might be a less attractive partner in the eyes of the supervisory directors. The highest bidder might even turn out within the not so long term to be less attractive with respect to employment, operations. Maybe the highest bidder is even planning to split up the company and sell it off.

An example is the typically Dutch company Stork. It has a relatively low price-earnings ratio. It could be a theoretical example. If Stork were now split up into several parts, the sum of these parts would generate a higher shareholder value than if Stork were left intact. I could imagine that a foreign company with hopes to acquire Stork would run into a lot of emotional resistance in the Netherlands – leading to the whole deal being called off.

In my opinion, an acquisition should always provide added value in the long term. A shorter-term vision is generally not good for the future of the company. That might result in a higher share price at that moment, with a higher price for the shareholders. But then they pull out and forget about the company because they have gone off to invest elsewhere this time. In this case, I'd rather see an acquisition with a longer-term plan for the company, that holds the company together (maybe with a few changes here and there) and that adds its own distribution network, for instance, as a means to increasing the return on operations. The highest bidder is not necessarily the best candidate.

In the US, too, one is not necessarily obligated to respond to the highest bidder. There are other values of which an organisation needs to take account. It is therefore not typically Dutch to include other stakeholders in their considerations. However, this discussion is more dominant in the Netherlands than in the US. That has to do with the form of protection we choose.

In Belgium, Fortis succeeded in striking a deal with Generale Bank, while ABN-AMRO failed. The latter concentrated on the incumbent management and thought it had a deal with them. But that was not so: the shareholders were the ones holding the reins, and they had other designs. That is also a type of protection. Germany has a system whereby large blocks of shares are held by merchant banks, the most traditional form of protection. Minister Zalm once said that he would like to get rid of those anti-takeover mechanisms, but that he would not have any objection at all if they were replaced with strategic blocks. They are therefore familiar with protection abroad too, but there that takes place via the shareholders. That means that if the present anti-takeover mechanisms were to exit the market, others will take their place.

A bill has been put forward according to which a 70% stake would have to be held for a year; after which the parties would have to ask the Enterprise Section of the Amsterdam Court of Appeal to neutralise the "shark repellent", so that the company can be taken over. The Enterprise Section will honour the request unless someone advances a weighty concern. I myself would like to qualify that somewhat. The onus of proof should rest with the party acquiring the company. That party should be required to prove that its plans are much better than those of the incumbent management. That would be fairer. I am also convinced that protective measures against hostile takeovers should absolutely not be taken solely for the purpose of protecting the present management. That's wrong. One often sees people hiding comfortably behind a wall in this respect.

At shareholders meetings we have repeatedly heard Isaac van Melle say that Mentos is a world-class brand and that many a person would like to have that brand and, other than that, leave Van Melle as it is. He has given examples of similar companies that have been bought up through the brand, only to disappear subsequently from the market, without any further chances. "Should we do that too?", he asked himself. "No," the shareholders cried. This time, there happened to be a representative present from the VEB who had many objections to the limited certification. And now he saw that the shareholders wanted something completely different from what his association had thought all along. At the same time, Van Melle is still producing good results. Nobody has anything to complain about. I should add that a company needs the peace and quite to choose its partners.

I am therefore not necessarily against anti-takeover mechanisms, unless they are used the wrong way. If you are at odds about that, you should go to court. I would like to see a reverse onus of proof included in the pending bill. I have been seeing a development where depositories and certification are diminishing. The possibility of preference shares remains; it does not really matter very much whether you place them with a foundation or somewhere else. With an increase in scale, one can afford to use somewhat less shark repellent. Nevertheless, I still think that strategic shareholders will take its place and that no one is willing to be caught off guard so easily.'

But would the Netherlands have ever had such large companies without anti-takeover mechanisms?

Prof. Glasz: 'People use that argument more often: why did ING acquire BBL and not vice versa? That's because the executive committee at ING had greater possibilities because of the anti-takeover mechanisms and such to think strategically and to expand the bank, while the people at BBL – as the story goes – did not have the time to expand the bank because of their differences in opinion. I don't know. Fortis and Generale have exactly shown that the protective measures against hostile takeovers in Belgium functioned perfectly.'

Aren't the anti-takeover mechanisms less absolute there? After all, Fortis was able to 'sign up' Generale Bank. They had too little power purely on the basis of the representatives of the shareholders. By winning over individual directors, they were able to succeed.

Prof. Glasz: 'That is now the big discussion in Belgium. But Dutch anti-takeover mechanisms also create risks. Without trust, a defence

131

mechanism does not give much protection any longer. As far as that is concerned, we are seeing the birth of a new culture in the Netherlands. Not only can a company's management be taken to court for supposedly holding back developments that would be in the interest of the company, or with an action to force them to negotiate with the plaintiff, but the officers of foundations can be taken to court as well. Here the action might have to do with them not being able to exercise their voting right on preference shares unless that is done independently. In that case they are seen as biased.'

How will the Fortis group develop? Capital markets are becoming international. All sorts of large-scale problems are arising.

Prof. Glasz: 'I assume that Fortis too will soon become larger – certainly in the US. I suspect that the Dutch banks will not limit their ventures to continental Europe. People have too much trust in the Americans and the British for that. That's been around since our liberation in 1945. We were not liberated by the French but by the British and particularly the Americans. My generation has not forgotten that. The present Americans naturally do not always come across as pleasant, but they are succeeding in this world. They are at least doing something. I was a member of the Dutch Upper House for twelve years and have seen a lot of legislation go by. And every time I thought to myself: is this really going to have any effect? Members of Parliament and the government are awfully proud of themselves every time they make a new law; but how that law is to be applied and whether it can be executed and whether it will really solve a certain problem or whether it will only create more problems – no, those are things that nobody thinks about. I therefore admire people who are able to put their money where their mouth is. That's why I'm also pessimistic about European co-operation. Very little is being accomplished. And whatever they do succeed in accomplishing still has to be embedded in the national legislation.

Now the question about the banks. What is their future? That's something that cannot be found in the legislation. Neither is the central bank inclined to say whether one should deal with the Belgians at this moment and who should exercise supervision over Fortis. There might come a time when people will have to leave that to a European institution. That's naturally something that the central bank needs like a hole in the head, since that would put its own existence in danger. That applies to all member states. But that is very different in the US. That is a mature federation. I'm afraid that Europe has a long way to go.'

Are you a proponent of a type of United Nations organisation for financial markets that regulates and intervenes? Should we tax financial flows to keep raids without a financial-economic basis from taking place on countries or regions? After all, that can lead to economic instability, such as we've seen again in the crisis in Asia.

Prof. Glasz: 'Once the international borders have disappeared, something will have to be done. What will we get instead? A free market? Well, then there's the risk of the major players running the show according to the law of the jungle. I do not trust the market completely. I find it cruel. One naturally needs to give the market the space to regulate itself. One must take advantage of healthy market influences, but it is recommended to guide it now and again before it becomes overheated or goes off the road. That will be more difficult as soon as the international borders disappear within a single Europe. And we can see what is becoming of Europe right now. To my mind, co-operation has been very disappointing in all sorts of areas. The big three – Germany, France and the UK – are still thinking in national terms. They see the world and therefore the rest of Europe in terms of themselves; the rest are simply expected to adapt. That's something I say boldly on purpose, but things still have not changed. Just take a look at the crisis in Kosovo and elsewhere. It's as if they just cannot succeed in developing a uniform policy. Maybe a supranational body should supervise the financial markets, but whether that will ever happen...'

Will the euro concept unify Europe?

Prof. Glasz: 'If the euro is an effective means of positioning Europe as a single block in the financial world against other financial trading blocks, it is a means that we should embrace. And that seems to have worked. Nostalgia about having our own currency – I don't see any business advantages in that. It will take some getting used to now that our Queen's face won't be on it anymore, but the Dutch aren't going to be that heart-broken.

The movement towards Europe as a single block seems a good idea to me. It would be good if Eastern European countries could join. The unification of Germany is also something I applaud. That has led to political stability. While it is naturally costing Germany a lot, its money and efforts have been put to good use. The more we share our wealth, the less envy and fewer breeding-grounds for instability we'll have and the greater the market will become. In short, everyone eventually has a lot of positive things to gain from it. That's where Germany is today. And if the euro can help them find that stability, then it's a good thing.'

Is the relationship between the academic and the business world mutually beneficial? Or are they two separate worlds?

Prof. Glasz: 'It's getting better. The universities have also expressed that improvement is necessary – even if that is only because they desperately need the business world's money. A university's job is to produce academics who are able to function in our society. That was lacking. This was something that they already realised in the US. That's why I also try to incorporate their practice into my lectures with case studies and such. That is not necessarily standard, but the students are beginning to get a feel for it. I have my students write a position paper. This was something completely new to them: coming up with a problem, taking their own perspective on it and drawing their conclusions – all in less than ten pages. They would like to write more, but no one would read that. The audience will read the conclusion at most. And it has to be ready the next day and be well thought-out too. In addition, they have to present their papers as well. That's something that the Dutch are not so good at. Ask a Dutch child what his name is, and you'll get a few unintelligible noises in response. Ask a child in the US what his name is, and he'll answer with more than you wanted to know, in clear and frank terms. The Dutch are afraid to do that. But it still has a strong effect; if you see how things succeed in politics and elsewhere solely on account of how they are presented – with the content being supplied afterwards – it becomes clear why the Netherlands does not come across so well internationally.

Presentation is very important. That's something else they should teach at the university: how to put one's thoughts into words and especially how to adapt to the world around us. I'm sometimes ashamed of how "Dutch" we are in our international activities and how much more we could achieve if we were more sensitive to other cultures. We always believe that others should learn to think our way. But that is not feasible, of course.'

12. Strategy is finance; finance is strategy

In conversation with Mr. J.H.M. Hommen

Strategy and finance are two disciplines that are increasingly growing towards one another. Where a distinction was usually made between the person who determined the strategy – normally the chairman of the Board of Management – and the person who was responsible for the operational finances, each strategy is now evaluated on its merits from a financial point of view. This concept is also referred to as Value Based Management (VBM). One of the companies that has opted for this is Philips. This multinational company is confronted every day with financially tinted challenges and problems, such as the financial crisis in Asia, corporate governance and the globalisation and computerisation of the financial markets. How is such a company managed? We asked this and other questions to Mr. Jan Hommen (1943), Chief Financial Officer of Philips.

Mr. J.H.M. Hommen

Mr. Hommen graduated from the Tilburg School of Economics in 1970 and joined an aluminium company as controller. In 1978, he became Assistant Treasurer Corporate Finance for this company in Pittsburg, where he was responsible for Corporate Finance and investor relations. In 1986, he was appointed Vice President & Treasurer and in 1991 was appointed Executive Vice President & Chief Financial Officer. He transferred to Philips in 1997. Since he took up office, Value Based Management has occupied centre stage.

VBM is a strategic financial decision-making and management model. It focuses on maximising the enterprise value in the medium to long term. With the aid of VBM it is possible to define the strategic choices that should increase the value of the company in the long term. VBM aims to guarantee the continuity of the company in the long term by creating and maximising shareholder value.

A company is only successful and only creates value if it generates more resources than the providers of capital require or, in other words, if the net operating profit after tax is better in the long term than the return that the providers of shareholders' or loan capital expect from their invested capital (weighted average cost of capital). Naturally, the risk profile of the company's activities are taken into account in this respect.

In order to effectively manage the organisation it is vitally important that the decision and performance standards are in alignment. A company's internal management system should therefore be directed towards the realisation of economic value and not towards the traditional concept of profit. With the introduction of VBM, it is made quite clear to managers and directors that money is not free. It forces them to thoroughly revise their strategy and assess whether each investment will yield sufficient a return.

However, VBM can only produce good results if the management and the various business units show commitment to the implementation and if information about markets and the financial status of the company is reliable and available in detail. It is therefore vitally important to ensure that the management is provided with insight into the value drivers and can apply these in practice.

VBM enables the company to prevent a gulf being created being the company's actual market value and the market value as imagined by the management. How is VBM implemented in practice at Philips?

Mr. Hommen: 'VBM is actually a tried and tested concept. At Philips we measure Economic Profit Realised (EPR). In this concept, all business units are assessed every month, every quarter and every year with respect to the "value" results they have achieved. At a company as large and complex as Philips this must be kept simple certainly initially. Only then is it possible for everyone to easily come to grips with it. We have therefore put one thousand of our line managers through our own Value Based Management course. This year (2000), we will really be using EPR. We are not yet entirely where we should be with VBM because the concept is still "trickling" through the organisation.

We have had to change our usual reporting, for instance, for goodwill depreciation and tax rates. The intention is to imitate the real cash flows as much as possible and then relate this to the real amount of capital invested in each of the eighty business units. We allocate the capital to our businesses while calculating the costs of that capital as accurately as possible for each unit individually. It is up to the businesses to try to achieve a return on capital that is higher than their cost of capital adjusted for risk. Each business unit has been allocated a risk factor in the capital costs.

We have opted for this method because we are of the opinion that value thinking and economic thinking are not always sufficiently developed. Too many people think that capital is free and doesn't cost anything. We also think that this concept is best suited to our objective to create shareholder value.

The initial phase has gone well and we must now start refining it. We will now give our staff departments, R & D for example, a model with which they can measure their added value. Hopefully we will thus be able to focus on those R & D projects that have the best chance of value creation. It's all about making clear whether we continue with the project or not; in this way resources are not wasted and can be used elsewhere. VBM is thus beginning to find a use here as well. It is a concept that holds good for the entire enterprise.'

So we mainly see VBM in the field of performance measurement? The evaluation, the calculation of bonuses?

Mr. Hommen: 'The main thing for me is the valuation of the strategy. We have now completed a phase of strategic planning which we have consciously measured with VBM. This is because we want to know which strategic options have value potential. That is calculated and the results are now being utilised. We also use VBM for the allocation of capital for projects and elements of them. Finally, we use VBM for the measurement of performance and the remuneration associated with it.'

An important measure is of course the Weighted Average Cost of Capital (WACC), which is determined by the financial structure. To what extent can the business units influence the relevant decisions of the group management? Do they have any freedom?

Mr. Hommen: 'Of course they have some freedom. For each company or business unit we calculate a WACC with an assumed capital structure for the activity in question. Philips Lighting is, for example, a stable part of the company with a stable cash flow. In this case there are no problems using a relatively high debt financing. But for those parts of the company which are involved with very advanced and constantly changing technology, where there are very rapid developments and where you must be continually prepared to put new money in the development or to finance new equipment or new patents or licences, I do not want to take any risk on my capital structure. The business risk structure is too vulnerable for this. In this area we have units that are financed with 10%, at the outside 15% and sometimes even 0% loan capital. It therefore depends upon the nature of the company. In addition, we try to calculate a risk factor per business unit which reflects the real risk of this unit as much as possible.'

The Philips hierarchy talks about value. What about at the lower levels?

Mr. Hommen: 'It is vitally important that everyone participates. Everyone is needed in this value creation process. For a large part of the company it is difficult to establish what the annual value contribution has been. In this case, the Balanced Scorecard, in which we combine the most important value drivers, can be of assistance. We translate some of these drivers into non-financial indicators, which, if they are properly determined, give a good indication of the value creation process in departments or even small workgroups. Everyone – a member of the Board of Management is no different from someone on the shop floor – should thus be able to measure how they contribute to the value process of the company as a whole.'

Who follows the VBM process in order to judge whether the one department works as hard as the other?

Mr. Hommen: 'You need management for this. Not centralised management, because you cannot manage everything centrally. No, the main objectives must be defined per business unit and it is then up to the management in question to optimise the value creation. It is the job of that management to determine how this is done. Furthermore, we perform audits and visit companies. Our financial departments ensure that the management has sufficient and timely insight into where and how much value is created.'

VBM is thus more than a passing fad?

Mr. Hommen: 'What is attractive about VBM is that it provides insight into whether and how everyone makes a contribution to increasing the value of the company. You will certainly see this improve if you work with changes in value per business over time. However, it should not be made absolute. It is just one part of the measuring process. It applies to the determination of strategy and the capital allocation and to regular results. Furthermore, we also keep up to date with return on equity and all kinds of associated data.'

Where financial statements are concerned, there has been discussion for many years about Economic Value Added. Stein-Stewart, for instance, wants to make 164 modifications to this model. How many do you apply?

Mr. Hommen: 'We apply three (goodwill, tax rate and capital costs per element) and determine whether a few should be added to make the picture "more complete". But in my experience, the more complicated it is the less appealing it becomes. We must remain understandable for people who are not well versed in finance. And there is a limit to how far you can go. Certainly where a large company is concerned.'

How are strategic financial decisions made in a company like Philips? Is it a spontaneous process or is there a fixed procedure?

Mr. Hommen: 'Most decisions are well prepared over a long period. The strategic plans for each division are regularly studied in great detail. This involves analysing what the possibilities and strategic options are, together with the proposals of the management and ultimately the decisions. We see a strategic plan much more as a compulsory guideline and we see the annual budget as a contract.

The strategy is determined by the businesses themselves, not by the enterprise. We do have a Corporate Strategy department within Philips, but this assists the businesses with the completion of the strategic process and ensures that the end result is clearly understood by everyone. This department also assists the Board of Management with the analyses of the business units' portfolio, determines whether co-operation is possible with other companies or business units and whether alliances with other external companies are possible.

We also have an M&A department that is responsible for the execution individual transactions themselves. This department prepares the sale, purchase or merger and in principle conducts the negotiations. The transaction may be such that we as general management take over responsibility and thus assist M&A, but this is only the case with major transactions. Polygram, for instance, was done by Boonstra and myself with the extremely capable assistance of M&A and a whole series of internal and external consultants.

We therefore have a department that maintains the relationships with investment bankers. This is sometimes assisted by a transaction team with lawyers, tax experts, accountants and other specialists that are required at the time. The team also includes people from the businesses themselves, from product divisions or from business groups that provide advice as required. Before we do something, the scenarios, plans and strategies are always analysed in detail and submitted to the Board of Management. Decisions which have a far-reaching effect on the share price of Philips or a third party are always first submitted to the Board of Management.

The preparation process is very intensive, as is the subsequent deployment process. In the past, it was possible that someone who really wanted to sell or buy something actually concluded the deal. This was not always a good combination. That's why we now arrange for the performance of a comprehensive due diligence, and involve the M&A department etc. Everything is analysed in full and no steps are taken until at least two members of the Board of Management have been to the company to be acquired, know the company, have spoken to the management, know what the consequences could be, etc. Emotional decision-making is no longer acceptable.'

What is currently the longest strategic plan?

Mr. Hommen: 'The plan with the longest time horizon should be complete in 2003.'

How does the problem of corporate governance manifest itself at Philips?

Mr. Hommen: 'At Philips we have excellent external supervisors. The segregation of duties is very clear: they do not interfere with the day-to-day management, but do want to know where we are going with the company or why we do things a certain way, what our objectives are and why this in particular and not another. In other words, it's all about asking the right questions in a constructive atmosphere. The supervisors obviously require justification and call us to account; but they always do this with the intention of correcting mistakes or avoiding them. If corporate governance is practiced in this way there will only be benefits.

Experience with corporate governance in the Netherlands differs somewhat from that in Anglo-Saxon countries. In the Anglo-Saxon world there is a tendency to only take account of the shareholder, while there is a much greater focus on the social component here. A balanced combination of both approaches is obviously better.

Corporate governance does not end with the relationship between the Board of Management and the supervisors; it runs right through the company itself. The staff must know where the responsibilities lie, where the reporting routes run, what must be submitted for approval and what can be delegated. This must be clearly defined. The general rules of conduct must be set down in a manual which everyone should have in their desk drawer or which can be retrieved electronically from the database using their PC. This can be very far-reaching, even including processes with respect to the use of e-mail.'

Who is responsible for business ethics at Philips?

Mr. Hommen: 'The Board of Management is responsible. It has appointed a committee which closely follows the policy in this respect. The committee tightens the criteria from time to time and at regular intervals the Internal Audit Department examines whether and how the rules are complied with. Since we are a multinational company active in many countries, the business ethics may differ somewhat from country to country. We take account as much as possible with the customs and traditions which predominate in the world. We naturally leave this to the local offices, but the Philips culture remains the guiding principle.

In China, we have wholly-owned subsidiaries and they must comply with our corporate standards and rules. Where joint ventures are concerned, this is rather more difficult. If you own less than 50%, you are unable to exercise complete control over the management.'

What is you opinion about the euro?

Mr. Hommen: 'Up until now, I am rather disappointed with it. The hope was that it would become a somewhat stronger currency, but this has not really happened. I had not expected it to drop so much. It therefore appears that the international community still has problems seeing the euro as a reserve currency and the dollar is still preferred to the euro.

Of course, I do understand that it is very difficult to introduce a new currency, but it is taking too long for the euro to become a real means of payment. The man in the street will not be confronted with it until 2002. I myself am a member of the EMU committee which would like to have the euro introduced everywhere. The number of euro transactions by large companies is still limited, although at Philips the percentage is high at about 40%. Nevertheless, the process is irreversible. It is just a pity that it will take so long for the euro to be introduced in full. If the notes and coins had been introduced earlier, the euro would have been stronger, I think. There would have been more demand for it for business transactions.'

Some say that a good currency can never be launched without political union.

Mr. Hommen: 'Things go wrong as soon as people start messing around with the basis of the euro – that is the Treaty of Maastricht – and changing the percentages for Italy, and subsequently complying with French demands. In the long run, I think everything will turn out alright. At the moment, I am more afraid of the fact that the German economy is underperforming. That's where the real problems are. Germany should be the economic driving force of Europe and its engine is misfiring.

If you compare the European economy with that of the US, it is striking how quickly the latter has recovered, how quickly reforms are introduced in that country, how well people have capitalised on Internet developments, for example, while Europe and certainly Germany is running behind and gasping for breath. I think that the mobility of the German economy is too low. It must increase to a higher level. I am not alone in this opinion: many German experts agree.

So the euro will be disappointing as long as the German economy shows weak performance and as long as the euro is not introduced in full. The more euro transactions are performed, the more quickly the currency will be accepted.'

How does a company like Philips deal with the crisis in Asia?

Mr. Hommen: 'The Asia problem was partly caused by western banks providing too much credit subject to very lenient conditions. This is a problem of banks that go to extremes; to the point where they can go no further. You then shouldn't be surprised if things go wrong. The growth of the Asian region has been very rapid, while governance has not developed at the same pace. What we have learned from the crisis is that there are a number of institutional limitations. These must be removed. Incidentally, this was also a revelation for the local governments, which were brutally confronted with the fact that they had to work in a different manner. It had to happen sometime.

At Philips, we tried to anticipate the problems and took the necessary measures. As a result, we were able to cushion the first blows. Nevertheless, if everything goes down, the effect is still clear however well hedged you are and then afterwards there are new circumstances to take account of. This means that you have to act quickly and adapt to the new situation.

We seized the crisis as a good opportunity to buy and to enter into alliances. All in all, such a crisis has had the effect of fluffing up the pillows. Quite paradoxically, it seems that a forest fire is even favourable for the forest as a whole: old wood is destroyed and soon seeds lying in the warm ash germinate and create a vigorous, new forest. The situation is no different in these kinds of cases. The weak and unsuccessful companies are thrown out and opportunities for new, dynamic companies are there for the taking. Strong, well-established companies like Philips are thus able to re-establish their entire network of suppliers and customers, or at least re-evaluate them. Of course, we must not underestimate the problems. We must be decisive and flexible in order to get through the difficult period as quickly as possible.

What a company should absolutely not do in such a case is to surrender its market position in panic just like that. We have seen examples of companies which pulled out and which will have the greatest difficulty returning to the market later on. We have stayed put in most places, although with fewer staff and at lower costs and the like. But we do not want to lose our hard fought market position because when Asia gets back on its feet in the future we want to be on board.'

It has been said that markets which are dominated by short-term thinking should be stopped, because they will otherwise become a plaything for speculators. Is Wall Street further in this respect than the European markets?

Mr. Hommen: 'I don't know, it seems that a couple of analysts on Wall Street who made negative comments about a particular share had an enormous influence on the prices. That is the risk if you have a limited float of shares or if your shares are not readily marketable or if only very few people follow your company. Therefore, if information is incomplete all kind of games are possible. Volatility could also increase if a relatively large number of options are written on the shares in circulation. However, you don't see this if a market is working properly.'

Should the control over global financial flows be improved?

Mr. Hommen: 'No, the free market is in itself a good regulator and it will eventually force the participants to make the right decisions. This mechanism may sometimes be disrupted, but this disruption does not usually last long. At the moment, people certainly have access to an enormous amount of information via all kinds of electronic channels. Unreliable information can therefore be invalidated much more quickly than in the past.'

As Chief Financial Officer of a multinational company, how do you regard the reduction in size of the banking landscape?

Mr. Hommen: 'A multinational company like Philips must try to ensure that as much of its financing as possible is channelled through the capital market. As a result, it develops a relationship with its financiers. Such a relationship is different from the often-personal relationship which it has with the banks. Banks are excellent for payments and currency transactions, for the provision of support facilities or complicated project finance and for facilitating commercial paper transactions. For long-term financing, I prefer the capital market, partly because it can often provide longer maturities, certainly if a company is an accepted credit risk in the market. Payment transactions, currency transactions, custodial activities are services which can best be provided by large banks. They have a larger scale and are able to charge lower costs. However, as a businessman I am rather wary of the dependence upon capital, certainly if it is only provided in the future by a few large banks. Nevertheless, there are still enough banks and money is the ultimate commodity; it is always available, it only has its price.'

Is the European stock exchange an absolute necessity?

Mr. Hommen: 'A European stock exchange could eventually be attractive. However, we see on the US market, for example, that the exchanges are imperceptibly specialising and are seeking and acquiring their own character. On the NASDAQ, for instance, we see many IT and technology companies. This is not a problem as long as there is sufficient liquidity on the exchanges. For Philips it is attractive to appear on as many indices as possible, the more the better. A major part of the capital is managed passively these days.'

After the turn of the century, what will the characteristics of a good financial director be? Should he be more of a computer specialist than a financial economist? And is there sufficient talent available in the Netherlands?

Mr. Hommen: 'I have been involved with the controllers course in both Tilburg and Maastricht as a member of the board of governors. These courses normally compete with one another, but for me it is vitally important that the Netherlands produces well-qualified financial people, the more the better. The financial function is changing rapidly. The demands imposed on companies' financial experts are fundamentally different than they were ten years ago. A company no longer needs people who look back to calculate what the past month's revenues have been. Good computer systems do this. People want to know what the earnings will be next month, next week, tomorrow and in six months time. They want to know what the decisive success factors are and how these can be controlled. They want clear answers to questions such as: What is the situation with respect to capital expenditure? In which areas are we lagging behind? Where should we be faster? How are our competitors faring? For which projects is more research and development required? And: How can we measure whether those kinds of projects have a chance of success? Management wants to know how quickly arrears can be made up, how quickly competitors can be beaten and how the life cycle of a product can be calculated.

To put it briefly, there is a demand for economists or financial experts who are able to participate in the thought process, who know the development path of a product, who know the market and understand something about technology. These are quite different from – with all respect – administrators or accountants who are only able to certify whether the financial statements tally.

We must have "scouts" who can think along with us. This means that the courses must be modified. Everyone should be able to have access to the information. In this respect, IT has enlarged the world for us. We can establish "knowledge management", which among other things means the setting up of databanks with connections to Dow Jones, Reuters or Bloomberg. The whole world lies at our feet.

At Philips we have set up an internal knowledge bank containing the names and other relevant data of Philips people at our sites all over the world who have specialised knowledge in a particular field; it doesn't matter whether this relates to the blowing of special glass or the development of software. When someone at one of our locations is faced with a specific problem which he does not immediately have an answer to at that moment, he can query the databank with a particular keyword and out roll the names and other relevant data. Those who sign up for inclusion in the databank are obliged to reregister every six months; if not, their name is deleted. In this way, our people have access to the enormous and fresh potential of Philips experts all over the world in the most diverse of fields.'

How does the system sift out intruders? Doesn't the databank sometimes contain sensitive information and company secrets?

Mr. Hommen: 'Where company secrets are concerned, there are people who know so much that they certainly have to be protected.

Financial data is also handled with care, certainly if it could be used for insider trading. But our own experts may certainly be given access to less sensitive company information. The more knowledge we can activate and distribute among our own people the better. In contrast to material commodities, knowledge is not scarce; by distributing knowledge it is possible to increase it. Here you see the old adage, that you can enrich yourself by giving to others, become reality.

Obviously, we do not want to make the competition any wiser than it already is and so the knowledge bank is only intended for Philips staff. We keep it within our walls, but if a Philips employee in Singapore requires some particular information which may be in the possession of a Philips employee in Brazil this can now be quickly passed on while this was previously inconceivable.

What applies to all positions within the company is that you have to know where the information can be obtained and how systems work and how information is processed. This therefore applies to the financial director who must have both financial expertise and be able to think strategically. He must therefore have more than one string to his bow. This may appear impracticable, but it has become feasible with the possibilities offered by IT. As I already said: IT has opened up the world to us and this opening up is a challenge to be investigated.'

13. The government may regulate, but the market rules

In conversation with Mr. P.M. Feenstra

While it may be true that all the institutionalised aspects of the euro are governed in Frankfurt, seat of the European Central Bank, London continues to be the European number one when it comes to capital markets investment banking, fund management etc. In Europe London is where the shareholder value, value based management and corporate governance is primarily determined and where financial markets or trends in mergers and acquisitions of financial institutions evolve. In his capacity as managing director and head of investment banking for the Benelux and Scandinavian region at Goldman Sachs, where he's been working since 1990, Mr. Pieter Maarten Feenstra (1957) is confronted with this fact each day.

Mr. P.M. Feenstra

Isn't shareholder value being slightly overrated nowadays?

Mr. Feenstra: 'Every self-respecting Chief Executive Officer and manager recognises the importance of shareholder value and knows it is an integral part of the "stakeholders" concept. All types of decisions, whether they are at strategic or operational level or activity driven, can no longer be made without taking careful consideration of the financial implications. Shareholder value has become an important indicator of corporate performance, which is a main driver of corporate decisions.

Shareholder value is an indicator that recognises that equity investors – i.e. investors who contribute their own capital – have different motives for making their investment decisions. A company must make a profit. If not, it will not have access to the capital markets. In addition, shareholder value helps realise equilibrium. For example, due to the notion

147

of shareholder value, the equity market is capable of making a clear distinction between short-term measures, which are not always beneficial to the company, and long-term measures which are.

The corporate world should not attempt to protect itself from the growing focus on shareholder value. Capital markets have opened up, a fact which the introduction of the euro as a single European currency will only stimulate and maintain. Even now, the research community has already made a clear switch from a country viewpoint to a European sector viewpoint. In other words, rather than invest on a country basis, there is a growing tendency to investing in sectors that are represented throughout Europe. Consequently, companies will no longer be compared with their traditional competitors, but rather with competitors within the sector across or even outside Europe. In the past, the performance of Dutch companies was basically compared with that of their Dutch competitors. The comparison framework was a national one. This is no longer the case. More and more, industry observers are starting to attempt to identify sectors, which are global from a market's point of view, e.g. health and personal care, aerospace, defence, electronics and associated components.

If a company operates on an isolated basis, either in the Netherlands or in another jurisdiction, focusing on local circumstances suffices. Nonetheless, companies are increasingly faced with global regulations, and investors that are also increasingly global. Listed companies, even those from the US, cannot dismiss their shareholders pushing them in one direction or another. In other words, it is quite irrelevant whether one does or does not agree with the concept of shareholder value; the market simply dictates its significance.

I must say that the "stakeholders" concept currently prevailing in the Netherlands is a good one. It implies that the company must bear in mind the customers, the suppliers, the employees as well as the shareholders. This is not easy to quantify. Unfortunately, shareholders, particularly Anglo-Saxon shareholders, want to see measurable units. For this reason, the remuneration of managers in the USA is determined by shareholder value. Whether such remuneration is paid out in stock options or otherwise, is a different matter.

Of course, there is theoretically a risk that managers try to unduly influence the value of the shares, as their reward depends on that value. Provided the company performs well and the manager does his utmost to operate the company in the most profitable manner, there is nothing wrong with this type of reward.

I don't believe that management can consistently abuse information with a view to manipulating share prices. Markets are efficient enough to unveil such motivations. Large companies in particular are faced with the interest of a great many parties: the consumer, the shareholder, the creditor, the financial analyst and many others. Nobody is capable of deceiving so many different experts for any length of time.'

What you're saying is that, ultimately, the market rules. But which market are you referring to? There is a growing gap between the financial markets and the real markets. Some believe the Asia crisis has proven this to be true. Should there be more government control of the financial markets so as to avoid panic reactions?

Mr. Feenstra: 'Perhaps once or twice, speculators have succeeded in causing a panic on the market in order to benefit from depressed share prices, currencies, etc. in the confusion that followed. But nobody is able to realise this time and time again. If a market is healthy in economic terms, it should be sufficiently transparent – which it is indeed, also helped by recent developments in ICT – to neutralise manipulations. It is virtually impossible to manipulate a market, let alone disrupt it.

I would like to remark, however, that the ICT has a side effect. Aside from the official economic flows, there are also the unofficial ones. On the one hand, unfounded rumours can now spread faster than ever before. On the other hand, there is also a lot more opportunity to refute such rumours.

Besides: five years ago, traditional valuation methods such as discounted cash flow were applied with new technologies. We are now faced with the challenge of finding an explanation for the discrepancy between the two values, i.e. market value and accounting figures, in a sector such as Internet. Nonetheless, as I said earlier, the market itself will ultimately find the equilibrium.'

Some – and these are influential people – suggest levying a minor tax on financial flows, with a view to slowing down the processes and forcing people to look before they leap into action.

Mr. Feenstra: 'In the UK, we have a take-over panel. This is an independent body operating along side the stock exchange, which takes action when certain trends appear to get out of hand. It doesn't, however, come charging in as soon as there is any sign of smoke. Central banks used to take immediate action when exchange rates did not develop favourably. And then? Within a short period of time, they would purchase enormous bulks of currency and use up all their ammunition.

As a consequence, the market would jump in. Bob Rubin, former US Treasurer always said: "Ensure that the economy is sound and then the exchange rate will be a reflection of that." The government should take action only when the market indicates that involvement is required. The government cannot rule the market.'

Don't you think the potential of the euro is being overestimated? After all, the euro fell below the dollar only shortly after its introduction.

Mr. Feenstra: 'At Goldman Sachs, we believe the euro has traded below its value (at the time of this interview). The weakness of the euro is partly caused by cyclic differences between the US and Europe. The ten-year euro/US interest rate spreads – i.e. the difference between the ten-year interest rate in dollars and in euros – has been the currency's key driver. As at today Goldman Sachs Research predicts that inflation in the US will rise by 0.6% more than in the euro zone. In other words, we believe interest rates will decrease by 60 basis points, which is 0.60%. It is justified to conclude that the value of the euro will rise in comparison with that of the dollar. It is expected that once activity in the euro zone becomes more pronounced, this will result in a thinner bond spread.

A different matter is that the European financial market indices are becoming increasingly important. The number of European tracking indices is growing. Examples are FTSE Eurotop, Eurostocks 50, S&P Euro, all of which are typical pan-European indices.

I believe the euro is capable of homogenising the different capital markets and improving the liquidity and transparency of those markets. The euro will allow and facilitate cross-border mergers and acquisitions. This is illustrated by the first pan-European retail offering: Deutsche Telekom issued a capital increase of 11 billion euro. Goldman Sachs was the lead manager in this process. In other words: the 11 billion euro capital increase was actually the first transaction to be offered to the public at large in all countries within the euro zone. The result was an overwhelming demand.'

Where would you position Europe as a financial power in comparison with the US and Asia?

Mr. Feenstra: 'From an economic point of view, the future development of the euro is relevant in this respect as well. A lot will depend on that. Moreover, there is very little history to an Asian or European financial block. This makes it somewhat difficult to assess the balance of power and how the market will react to these three "blocks".

I myself believe – as many do – that the US will retain its leading position in the marketplace for quite some time to come. US Corporate Finance technology is far more developed than in the other blocks. Furthermore, US capital markets are "deeper" and the concept of shareholder value is more advanced.

I do want to point out that there is nothing to prevent a possible convergence of blocks in the long run. Capital markets have become more transparent and more liquid. There are a growing number of alternatives for investing and attracting capital. Besides, investors and all those who are active in the market have become far more professional.

More than ever before, capital markets now offer alternatives for investing as well as alternative capital structures and financing. On the other hand, the market for corporate control is less important than it was about ten years ago. Nowadays, mergers and acquisitions that bring about a synergy effect are more likely to be considered from a strategic standpoint and in relation to global efficiency. In the past, mergers and acquisitions were often financial transactions or leveraged buy-outs (LBOs), aimed at benefiting from undervalued assets. Besides, investors have more options than ever before to put their capital into various companies in various ways. I see this as a positive trend. The euro will certainly have an impact in this respect as well, as it will make the capital markets more homogenous and increase their liquidity. The market will also become more transparent. Exchange rates will no longer get in the way.'

All that may be true, but if countries like Italy fail to stay in line with the monetary terms, there will never be a strong European currency and, consequently, no political union.

Mr. Feenstra: 'On the contrary, we expect that it will happen sooner or later. Exactly because Italy has been included in Euroland, there's a good chance it will be realised. Much more so than if Italy had been excluded. Therefore, we expect that the yield differential between the euro and the dollar will decrease in future, causing the euro to increase in value in comparison with the dollar.'

But no matter how you look at it, the strength of the euro will depend on the strength of the German economic motor.

Mr. Feenstra: 'Yes, that's true to a certain extent. On the other hand, a single currency can take away so many inefficiencies that the advantages will outweigh the disadvantages. Exchange rate differences will be a thing of the past, where the former currencies of the euro countries are concerned. Importing or exporting companies will no longer be kept in doubt until their suppliers or customers either deliver or purchase, with time ticking away while exchange rates fluctuate.

Another advantage may be that countries which once had difficulty getting their economy straightened out will be able to achieve better results when there is a single bank to regulate. And yes, Germany does indeed play a key role in this respect.'

Should a single European stock exchange be a priority issue?

Mr. Feenstra: 'Stock exchanges are increasingly seeking to join forces with each other. Some experts are in favour of mergers, with strong arguments if I might say. These signals indicate that there is a desire for a single European stock exchange, which could have local representations. This also reflects the ambition of a pan-European capital market. Actually, it is a logical consequence of the euro.

By the way, there are many reasons to believe a convergence is already under way. The three stock exchanges of the Benelux had already signed an agreement in December 1998, for the creation of an integrated trading platform. Negotiations concerning a European stock exchange are in progress, although I am not aware of any results yet.

A single European stock exchange would also be very beneficial to medium and small sized companies. This sector would increase its European mindedness and find more opportunities to grow, as the market is larger. The European market will become their home market.

Perhaps this would enable a European "midcap", which would be welcome. However, such things take time. The first step was the EMU and its euro, which took a great effort. The second step is a single European stock exchange. In the future, an Italian investor, for example, will not only consider Italian shares but will also be interested in investing in Dutch, German or French companies. If there were a European midcap stock exchange, this would be much easier. But it won't happen overnight. It will take time and we have to give the process the time it needs.

In this respect we also have to let the market follow its own path. In due course, the demand will emerge from investors and companies.'

Is there any relationship between corporate governance and the value of a company? Does corporate governance create value within and for a company?

Mr. Feenstra: 'I really don't think we, in the Netherlands, should suddenly adopt the Anglo-Saxon system. We have grown accustomed to the way companies are structured in our country; how they are governed and protected from take-overs. While you have to stay in line with global trends rather than isolate yourself as a small country, this does not mean we should rush into a totally different corporate culture.

In this respect, the market will direct the way. I don't believe that an organisation can or should dictate corporate governance with a new set of rules. It just doesn't work that way. If the markets demand a certain type of corporate governance, it will simply happen. Every company competes in a global marketplace, not only for products but also for capital and reputation. At a certain point, the market will make the desired change quite clear. There isn't a government around that will be able to direct the outcome.'

How does a company like Goldman Sachs make its major strategic financial decisions? Does it follow an ingenuous procedure? Or is it behavioural finance? Do you work with models?

Mr. Feenstra: 'That depends on which decisions we are faced with. Some decisions concern internal organisational matters. Other decisions concern the client. Goldman Sachs does not deliver only one product: we are active in the fields of investment banking, equity sales, fixed income and commodities.

We have always been a partnership. In a partnership like ours, the partners are also the firm's shareholders. Important decisions are made within the partner group, by an executive committee. This is a very efficient method. We have historically always been a partnership and have always been accustomed to a direct approach: effective, focus on results, short lines etc. Recently, we became a public company and were listed on the stock exchange.'

Was the decision to go to the stock market based on subjective motives? Or was it just the most logical step, based on objective and scientifically supported indicators?

Mr. Feenstra: 'There were many motives. Many of our competitors were expanding and being listed on the stock exchange. There was a growing need for permanent capital. Being dependant on a limited number of partners is a solid basis, but attracting funds from third parties is even better. That provides an even stronger basis. The extra capital can be used to finance acquisitions, for example. In the past, when we were considering a take-over, the money had to be collected from the partners. Now, if we are contemplating a major acquisition, we can issue new shares to finance the deal.

And last but not least: a company like ours is entirely dependent on its staff. Our people are our most important asset. We wanted to realise a situation in which the ownership was more widely divided. Now, thousands of employees are shareholders of Goldman Sachs.'

Did Goldman Sachs set up a system of Value Based Knowledge Management for itself?

Mr. Feenstra: 'We work with transparent systems and there is a lot of communication. We can't do without it; knowledge and experience has to circulate effectively. So, we ensure that our people can communicate with each other day and night. The more we register and pass on signals to the right person, the better the results. One person may hear of something, the second may notice a certain trend, the third may have read something interesting and the fourth may invent a new concept. We keep close tabs of the knowledge available in-house and where we can find it. On the one hand, this is our corporate culture, on the other, we closely monitor what goes on in the world.

Knowledge has to be shared and distributed. Isn't it true that in many companies each employee is busy building his or her own little empire? Colleagues are purposely kept uninformed to improve one's own position. We don't want any such walls within our organisation. We have designated staff to keep the enormous database up to date, check conflicts and assess whether certain data can be passed on to clients. After all, it is in their interest to be well informed, without receiving redundant information.

Over the past ten years, we have also been confronted with clients who increasingly ask expert questions. We cannot pull the wool over their eyes. Clients also make their own analyses. Clients certainly don't have a short-term focus by wanting to make a quick profit; no, they are increasingly focusing on the long term. Clients are also increasingly aware of the fundamentals of investing.'

Over the past years, there have been a growing number of mergers among financial institutions. Is this good news?

Mr. Feenstra: 'If it helps improve efficiency and client focus, I believe it is a very good trend. Companies have to be large enough to bear the burden of certain investments, for example in costly IT systems.

And here again – I may become repetitious – certain trends are irreversible. I will try to illustrate this. Say a Dutch bank has 6 million Dutch customers. Given that the entire population of the Netherlands is 16 million, this is an excellent market share. But with the introduction of the euro, the area will encompass over 200 million people. Now where does that leave a company with only 6 million customers? So, even if a company doesn't want to merge or join forces, the economic situation dictates its necessity. Of course, mergers are far less complicated on paper than in reality. The expansion does have to be beneficial. The improved efficiency does have to be feasible and the different corporate cultures do have to fit in with each other. If not, the whole thing will be counterproductive. For all those involved, it should be obvious that the merger or alliance is imperative.'

What should a strategic finance expert know in order to perform optimally after the year 2000?

Mr. Feenstra: 'Do you mean in which field? I expect that Internet banking will become very important. But I don't know how the banks will react to that.

I do know that investing in IT will continue to be an absolute necessity. Yet, robots will not be able to replace human beings; human contacts, human ingenuity and creativity will always be key. When large or important clients choose Goldman Sachs, they do not do so because we are so well "automated" but rather because we have experienced staff who deliver sound advice. No computer could ever match that.'

14. Living from money: not for money

In conversation with Mr. H.H. Meijer RA

'Mammon wins his way where seraphs might despair,' is how the British poet Byron characterised the power of money. We have always been taught that money does not make us happy and the British comic Merton Glade proved this as follows: 'A man with ten million is no happier than a man with nine million.'

'You must live *from* money and not *for* money', comments Mr. Haddo Meijer RA (1944), vice-chairman of the Executive Board of Royal Nedlloyd.

Mr. Meijer: 'An organisation should optimise shareholder value by being competitive on the labour market, the sales market, the purchasing market and also the capital market. Shareholder value must not be a goal in itself. As soon as shareholder value is place in a broader framework, value can increase. People are quite indifferent about shareholder value in a company, but they are interested in the

Mr. H.H. Meijer RA

successes that are achieved, in working in teams, in major challenges. That's what people are involved in.

Financial experts have the tendency to set a measure for everything, to tune things. But does that produce much of a result? If you control an entrepreneur too tightly, there is no room for creativity, to improvise or to change course in good time. The entrepreneurial spirit should be supported. Models can always be used to show how things should be done, but the decisive factor is whether a product arrives at the customer the day after tomorrow in good time. Expressed in tautological terms, this is the reality.

It reminds me of the old balance sheet theory, which states that the balance sheet should have a prospective character because of the connection with the discussion about the theory of replacement value.

That is unnecessary, isn't it? There are countless techniques for looking towards the future. You must not let the balance sheet project something that it cannot generate. There are other tools for doing that.'

What about shareholder value from Nedlloyd's perspective?

Mr. Meijer: 'Nedlloyd has, quite appropriately, gone through a sea of change. When I started working here a few years ago, the company was facing severe financial problems. In order to get a grip on the developments I convinced the management that we had to drop the idea that the operating result was a good measure for financial performance. The result was subsequently redefined in terms of business result, after deduction of capital charges and business cash flow. Secondly, we attempted to reduce the capital employed. In other words, shake out money from your debtors and burden the profit and loss account as little as possible with capacity costs. As soon as the capacity costs are reduced, the invested capital decreases. It's all about the relationship between cost control and the control of the capital invested by means of achieving a target of a 10% return on the capital invested and realising a positive cash flow (after deduction of capital charge). This is what the management can be held accountable for. However, we have made clear that a temporary negative business result must be accompanied by a positive business cash flow. In this way, the management is forced to undergo a change in culture and think differently about level and use of the capital invested.

It is vital that straightforward and clear objectives are formulated. That is the reason why I said that the cost of capital should amount to 10% when I joined this organisation. The response to this was that the cost of capital would not be 10% at that time. No, of course not. I knew that as well. To avoid losing valuable time, it was not the 10% that was negotiable but the pace at which measures were to be implemented.

The pace at which changes can be introduced is something that is not given sufficient weight when matters are being considered, let alone the pace at which they can produce a result. Therefore, expensive management time must not be paid to a discussion about a particular percentage, but you should choose a percentage – in our case that was 10% – that the organisation can consider as a challenge and that is feasible. The 10% that we set was chosen because everyone could calculate in their head what the deficit was. The people had to confront themselves with their deficits and make their own sums. A perfect definition is not needed for that.

If I, as brand-new turnaround manager, had immediately started off with complicated models, with all kinds of value drivers and other professional, but theoretical artillery, I would have unintentionally been dragged into a debate about the perfection of my model; and about whether I had forgotten something or not. I did not want to get embroiled in that because who would then have had all the problems on his shoulders? Everyone would then have stood around to see how I would wriggle out of that. And that is not what it was about. It wasn't me, but the managers who had to think about improving the entrepreneurial approach.

Discussions about perfect definitions so often prevent rapid decision-making. It is important to take the first step as quickly as possible on the basis of your vision. The subsequent steps then follow automatically. As soon as the discussion degenerates into endless consideration about which steps must be followed, valuable time is wasted. During the implementation so much changes and you learn so much that the following step automatically announces itself as it were. You must have the nerve and that's what many economists have to wrestle with.'

Value Based Management starts by keeping a tight grip on capacity and only using what there is?

Mr. Meijer: 'Yes, that's right. The essence of our message was not to grow too fast because we would otherwise get into difficulties with the business cash flow. As long as the business result is negative, you cannot grow and you must even reduce capital invested, otherwise you can never finance the business result deficits. Value Based Management starts by keeping a tight grip on the capacity and deploying it efficiently. It is tempting to invest in order to show exactly what the organisation is still able to do, but I would argue in favour of restraint. There must first be a workable margin. If a company grows too fast with a margin that is too low, the end result is failure.'

Nedlloyd was a company with a wide range of activities. You had to ensure that these activities achieved a higher profit level. How did you tackle this strategically?

Mr. Meijer: 'Strategic thinking based on loss-making positions is difficult. We had established what our most important core businesses were: container traffic and European transport. All other activities were not part of core business. We therefore disposed of some activities, but then in a strategic manner and from a position of strength. That had to be done first by means of a turnaround operation.

We have changed the agenda because our ambition was for the company to achieve a top position on the European distribution market. We really thought this was possible until the post companies in Europe started to focus on our distribution activities. Our origins were in the truckload business and warehousing, and we had already moved in the direction of logistics. When we saw the strength of the post companies, which were assisted by strong financial positions enabling them to realise their logistics ambitions, we decided not to get involved in a fight. It was impossible for us to achieve such a top position in a responsible manner as there would have entailed too much risk for our organisation. The risk would also have been too great where shareholder value was concerned. That's why we threw in our lot with Deutsche Post, the ideal partner for us with the same vision of the future. This has led to the acquisition of European haulage companies with our top people, from the European transport operations, gaining key positions at Deutsche Post.

At Nedlloyd lines, the container traffic company, we also changed tactics. In 1995, when we had to issue the profit warning and were confronted with an enormous deterioration in rates, we first decided to increase the scale of our operations because we were not large enough to play the game. The economy of scale value driver is enormous. That was our reason for merging our shipping activities with those of P&O on a 50-50 basis. Together we have created the basis for the building of a megacarrier, a company that can transport about 5 to 6 million

Royal Nedlloyd Use of proceeds	
No	Yes
– Buy out of P&O Nedlloyd – Passive investment company	– Limited amount for possible strategic step P&O Nedlloyd? – Other alternatives possible? – Distribution to shareholders
⟶ Clarity end of 1999	

Table: Strategic options

containers each year. We are now carrying about 3 million, so we still have to double the size of our operations.

When I joined the company we had about 25,000 people on the payroll. We have always had two things in mind: how do we achieve sufficient shareholder value and how can give our people a future? Now that all the employees are accommodated with top strategic players, we can concentrate fully on shareholder value. In the past there was no contradiction between these two aspects because we sold everything strategically. If we have followed the bankers' recommendations at the beginning of 1993, we would have come nowhere near to realising the value that we have now. We asked the bankers to follow us and that's what they did. By buying strategically, we have also served the share-holders' interests.'

So if this turnaround operation had not succeeded, it wouldn't have been possible to play this strategic game?

Mr. Meijer: 'That's right, that had to be done first. You cannot negotiate strategically if you make losses. We have indicated to our shareholders what we will do and what we will not do with the cash that has been generated. We will indicate what the position is sometime near the end of 1999. The allocation of the cash is shown in the follow-ing flow diagram.'

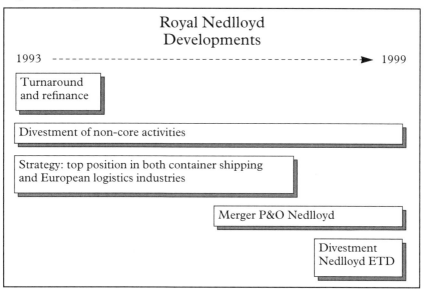

Table: Allocation of cash

Now you no longer have any major activities under your care, which position do you hold at Nedlloyd?

Mr. Meijer: 'I hold two positions, I am Deputy-Chairman of the Executive Board of Royal Nedlloyd and CFO of P&O Nedlloyd. We know exactly what is transported each week. We closely follow the development of tariffs and container flows and we know our liquidity position. Once every 4 to 5 weeks we have a thorough insight into the development of the result, into capital invested, prospects and the underlying performance indicators. Almost all investment decisions are taken centrally. Within the organisation, one of my posts is chairman of the investment committee, which naturally keeps an eye on the relationship between investments and strategy.'

How do you prepare for major investments? Is this based on discounted cash flow or are new techniques applied?

Mr. Meijer: 'This company is exceptionally capital intensive. Therefore, my first concern is not to grow too fast and to keep the capacity under control. On top of this, you must bear in mind that ships have a long life, as much as 25 years. It therefore takes almost three management generations before a ship has to be refurbished. In this respect, it is also very important how the old business economics principles take root: how is the capacity consecutively developed and how is it simultaneously developed? It is so easy to increase capacity simultaneously at the expense of the consecutive capacity. You need to watch this very carefully, because there is also a cycle where the prices of ships are concerned. In addition, it is vitally important to properly control the capital costs associated with the ships.

The question then arises whether you keep on reproducing your existing services or whether you have a look at alternatives you can generate. What you absolutely must not do is just keep on investing without change along existing lines. You should first properly determine what the options are and what mix of trade lanes you want to be involved in, for whom and with whom. That's a sign of business acumen.

You can consider options. That fits well in the strategic plan, particularly if you examine your product profitability linked to your investment profile. When we had to choose between a merger with the former Global Alliance or the former Grand Alliance we had two criteria in mind: the quality of the service – thus which ports we put in at and with which frequency we sail between the Far East and the US, for example – and how much capacity is created by this choice and which choice makes the least possible claim on the future cash flows. In this way you try to control the effects that your decisions have on the capacity in the industry. You must not forget that the addition of capacity is a risk factor in view of tariff developments. P&O Nedlloyd is a single large operating company that is managed by an Executive Committee, assisted by committees that prepare the decision-making. The most important committees are: Management Development, Planning, Investment, Systems, Sales & Marketing policy. The latter is concerned with product definitions in order to improve the profiling of our products for the customers. We are therefore both strategically and operationally active. If you look at the size of this operating company – turnover of about $4 billion and 10,000 employees – and bear in mind that we also hire additional capacity, you can assume that we have capital invested of about $4 billion (including ships on order). The capital turnover is therefore not much greater than one, so you can see how important it is to monitor the capital invested.

On top of all this, the question is how the best cargo base in the market can be achieved. This, together with the trade lanes, are actually the value drivers. To what extent do you own actions in the field of capacity influence the stability in the field of tariffs? This is a major problem in the container-shipping field: tariffs can very easily drift into a downward spiral if the players are too aggressive.

Container shipping is a commodity product and as long as there is sufficient capacity our customers do not have to be in doubt about the continuity of the logistic chain because the capacity is readily available. As soon as capacity becomes tight, the customer sees the vulnerability of such a logistic chain and must think about the continuity of services, as is also the case within the context of the millennium transition.

Since 1995, the capacity has increased much more rapidly than the demand. At the same time, the demand in the field of container shipping has grown fairly rapidly: about 21/2 times the growth rate of the world economy. If we then consider the shareholder value and look at the volume, we see that since 1995 the supply has been much greater than the demand, particularly on account of the ambitions of a few players in the Far East. We already saw that things had to go wrong, and that's exactly what happened. The supply of tonnage is now once again less than the development of demand. It takes one and half years before a ship that has been ordered is ready for service. We therefore have sufficient capacity until the end of 2000, but are keeping our finger on the pulse for the subsequent period.

In the past, container carriers still ordered five ships at a time, because the price per ship is then less. That represented an enormous investment, certainly at the ship prices then prevailing. So what happened? The new capacity came onto the market in spurts and the carrier in question had to make five ships profitable. They could have consciously accepted the underutilisation loss and gradually have filled the capacity in order to prevent tariff erosion. But what often happened was that such a carrier sailed below the market. The three largest alliances in the world have more than 40% of the world shipping capacity and have a stabilising effect on the growth of capacity. Are we now moving towards a more stable balance? What is the challenge that the industry actually faces? Can we succeed by means of consolidation? That is important because cost gains and discipline are realised in this way, certainly if the capital market – and with that I return to shareholder value again – also has a say.

Things could easily have turned out differently. We have become 30% cheaper. When we started, we were at $2000 per TEU on average. We have now dropped to $1300 per TEU, $700 lower. A simple calculation: about $3million TEUs × 700 = $2.1 billion tariff erosion against current turnover of $4 billion. Therefore, if circumstances had stayed the same, we could have had a turnover of $6 billion and $2 billion more profit. This is just to give you an idea of what the real strategic problem is in this business, i.e. control over revenues and scale.'

What are your ideas about corporate governance?

Mr. Meijer: 'We were very happy with the recommendations of the Peters Committee. If your carry responsibility you must also be prepared to be held accountable. The question is how you want to carry that responsibility. In our 1997 annual report we gave account with respect to the 40 recommendations of the committee. A number of recommendations were not followed and we provided reasons for this.

NedLloyd has a system of "one share, one vote". We abolished the voting right restriction. The most important objective of the "Stichting Prioriteit" (the body holding the priority share) is to control the company's cash-out and the shareholders cannot ask us to pay more dividend than this body allows.

You must be able to remain responsible for the liquidity and solvency of the company. At the end of the day I think it would be going too far to give the shareholders a say in what goes on in the company. Furthermore, they certainly do not have the competence to do that; the management is empowered to do that. The essence of investor relations is that the investor has confidence in the company and the management does not betray this confidence. Account must be adequately rendered by means of the associated communication channels.

I think that the regime applicable to dual-board entities that we have in the Netherlands is a good system of governance because it attempts to find a balance between capital and employment. You cannot leave it up to the shareholders to decide exactly what should happen, but you do need their support.'

Should shareholders be given more power to appoint or discharge managers?

Mr. Meijer: 'I am still in doubt on this point. I have no problem being held accountable to the people who invest in us. In the shareholders' meeting you often see people who only have a few shares. I respect the fact that they want to make use of their voting right, but on the other hand... If in-depth discussions about a particular policy have to take place, it has to happen with significant shareholders who know what they are talking about. If you look at the situation in the US, where you have "proxy solicitation", you see that the shareholders' meeting takes fifteen minutes. The decisions have already been put forward in advance. How many are in favour and how many are against? Next item! And there is absolutely no accountability towards the shareholders' meeting. We are therefore faced with a remarkable situation on that point. I recognise that the shareholders play an important role, I recognise that it is essential to be held accountable, but I do not think that a shareholders' meeting as we know it is a suitable vehicle within the context of corporate governance.

I would not have any problem accepting greater influence on the composition of the supervisory board or executive board. My worry is the one-sidedness with which it could take place. All the capital in the world is not incorruptible either. A feeling of responsibility is essential, but at the same time there must be a willingness to be called to account. It's all part of the same game.'

Discussion is raging in the Netherlands about management options at the moment. How should they be prudently dealt with? Should the rights be included in the financial statements?

Mr. Meijer: 'I think so, but the question is how. I am in favour of remuneration according to the relative performance in the industry, not on the basis of rising share prices. It's all about whether you do better than the competition.

Incidentally, I wonder whether a management option as such can be an incentive for your achievements and your judgement. For me personally it is much more important to achieve something which I can be proud of. My motives and incentives for performing optimally are therefore pride, satisfaction and sense of responsibility and not options.

If you are young you have many years in front of you and usually little money. As you get older, "years" become scarce and capital increases. At the end of the day, what do you actually need? Healthy years or money? I think the former. In other words, as the years go by money loses its importance in one way or another. My grandfather often used to say: "You must live *from* money, but you mustn't live *for* money." And if he was angry, he would say: "What do you want money for? Even dogs won't eat it." I often think about what he said. I have a Calvinistic opinion on the subject: the reward must not be too great. But once again, the rewards in some sports and in the field of entertainment are out of all proportion. The generally accepted view is different, however. If someone provides entertainment and amusement, it is quite all right, but if someone with exceptional qualities, who is prepared to work eighty hours a week, makes a contribution to the continuity of a large organisation and thus prosperity, we suddenly have a different opinion. Remarkable.'

Some people are very enthusiastic about the euro. Nevertheless, the euro cannot develop properly if there is no political unity in Europe. Do you agree?

Mr. Meijer: 'I see things differently. The preparation for the introduction of the euro has led to a reorganisation of public authority budgets and that is the first major benefit. The result is an enormous economic advantage, which we can scarcely overestimate. The euro is good for employment in the long term. That's where the challenge lies for the EU. I do not want to be pessimistic, but if we do not succeed in finding work for the young generation, there is a great danger that major social tensions will occur and that the political support for the euro will be threatened. Young people who are never given a chance to make their mark in society will use their energy in the wrong way. Young people, wherever their origins, must be found work, otherwise major, unmanageable problems will occur.'

How does a chartered accountant become a strategic financier?

Mr. Meijer: 'In my experience, as business economist and accountant, I have always been surprised about the differences between the two disciplines. There is often a confusion of tongues between economists and accountants within companies. Economists are unable to win over the accountant and the accounts do not provide the management information that is required to manage companies. As a business economist, I therefore started to study accountancy as well. Not with the idea of ever becoming a practising accountant, but just because I thought it was an essential course.

My criticism of accountants is that they focus on the financial statements as commodity product, while the business community is continually struggling with adequate management information. And the accountant is still unable to meet the customers' wishes in this respect. Consultants are therefore called in, while accountants are better able to judge management information; obviously as long as they want to communicate with the management on the right wavelength. The message must be put across clearly. It's all about providing management information. That is where the accountant can add most value. The capacity to do that is scarce, as is the creativity and the guts that are required.

My criticism of accountants is that they have focused for too long on the financial statements as a commodity product, while the business community is continually wrestling with adequate management information in a dynamic environment.'

15. Big, bigger, too big?

In conversation with Mr. W.M. van den Goorbergh

The Spanish writer Melchior de Santa Cruz is alleged to have once commented 'Not everything that is big is good, but everything that is good is big'. It certainly is the case that too big can be a handicap, or can become one. We also see this in the business world. How often does it happen that merged companies, lumped together into giant conglomerates, become so unwieldy and heavy that their only salvation is unbundling and slimming down? Nevertheless, in the banking world mergers and acquisitions are still taking place at an unrelenting rapid pace. The growth has apparently not yet come to an end. Contemplation with Mr. Wim van den Goorbergh, member of the Executive Board of Rabobank Nederland.

Mr. W.M. van den Goorbergh

Mr. Van den Goorbergh (1948), econometrist, obtained his doctorate in 1978 with Professor Schouten with the thesis 'A macro-economic theory of employment'. On 1 April 1980, he joined the Rabobank as 'adviser to the Executive Board' and in 1993 became member of the Executive Board.

He was involved in the establishment of Rabobank's international network. In 1986, he switched to the securities side of the Rabobank where he held various positions in the field of retail securities, issue activities and institutional clients. Later on, the bank's treasury function was added. In 1993, he was appointed to the Executive Board with domestic operations as his main responsibility. Since May 1999, he is Chief Financial Officer and Risk Manager within the Executive Board.

Will the merger trend, the growth of mega-banks, increases in scale, ever come to an end?

Mr. Van den Goorbergh: 'There is a number of driving forces behind the ongoing trend towards consolidation. First of all, there is the growing size of the global financial markets in which supply and demand of capital meet. This is the world of share issues, bond activities, of mergers and acquisitions, the world of investment banking. This world is highly dominated by US investment houses. Size is very important in this area and we have to assume that eventually only a very limited number of mega-players will remain.

Secondly, the concept of "all finance services", the clustering of banking activities with insurance and asset management, is becoming much more effective. In Europe this clustering is now in a process of being completed within the national boundaries and it is now beginning to take place on a supranational level.

Thirdly, there is the effect of information and communication technology on existing structures, means of operation and distribution formulas. The power emanating from this has an enormous influence on the financial world. The investments involved will play an important role in the considerations to proceed with the consolidation process.

We can establish that size is a more determinating factor in the area of relatively simple products and services. A credit card, for example, is an exceptionally simple product, both from the perspective of the provider as well as the consumer. Increases in scale can have a positive effect here. It has considerable advantages in terms of cost per unit, the use of systems, accessible twenty-four hours a day, etc. The same applies to straightforward facilities in the field of payments, savings and the like. Size is a very important factor here.

On the other hand, there is another world of financial services: that of more complex services like pensions, investments, personal financial planning, lending to companies, lease activities and so on. It is important here that the financial service provider has tailored solutions cut to the exact need of the customer. Therefore, we also see individual tailoring and small-scale activities close to the customer.'

And do we see this at the Rabobank?

Mr. Van den Goorbergh: 'We are an organisation that is rooted in and has grown out of local, relatively autonomous Rabobanks, which operate in their own area. At the same time they are organised in a central organisation responsible for the facilities and support of those local member banks. Our group also comprises activities in the field of asset management, in the field of insurance and on the global financial markets, which require considerable scale because of their nature.

We probably will have to scale-up these activities to a higher level in the European context. We could link up with other financial service providers in Europe that have the same nature as the Rabobank Group – strong on their own domestic market, strong customer focus, with relevant shares in the domestic market. Specialised services in the field of insurance, asset management, operations on financial markets can be brought on the European level by clustering activities. At the same time we maintain that fine-meshed network of contacts with customers on our home market. In this way the Rabobank Group connects both tendencies.'

With BBL, ING covers the Benelux, in the same way as Fortis does with Generale Bank, VSB, ASLK and Mees Pierson. Rabobank and ABN AMRO seem to remain behind. Shouldn't a financial services group like the Rabobank Group at least have the Benelux as its home market?

Mr. Van den Goorbergh: 'Don't overestimate the strength of the Benelux. The economic relationship between the Netherlands and Germany is probably a lot more relevant than that between the Netherlands and Belgium. The final destination of co-operation on the European level can never be the Benelux. Much more interesting is whether relationships between Dutch financial institutions and parties in France and Germany are possible. Where the European market is concerned, those two countries are the ones with the carrying power in Europe. Only the financial groups which at least also cover France and Germany can be said to really have a European dimension.'

Dutch banks have limited success stories in the German market.
Is it a difficult market?

Mr. Van den Goorbergh: 'It is a difficult market. Up until now, the operations of Dutch banks in Germany have generally not been very successful. This is connected with the hardly impenetrable structure of the German market, which is much less open than the British or American, for example. This has, in part, to do with the regulations in Germany and partly with the mentality of the German people.

Incidentally, we should be aware of the fact that the Dutch need other countries more than they need us. Where scale is concerned, small countries like the Netherlands have a much greater need than large countries like Germany or France. Dutch banks are therefore much more active in this respect than French or German ones and this puts a specific emphasis on the European strategy of all Dutch financial institutions.'

171

Won't the formation of gigantic banks frustrate the effective operation and competition in the financial sector?

Mr. Van den Goorbergh: 'Despite the trend towards concentration in the financial sector during the past fifteen years, competition has never been as intense as it is now. In my opinion, the cause is the "all-finance" concept. Previously the banking world was much more segregated: NMB served self-employed traders and small businessmen, Rabobank served farmers, ABN was for companies with many international activities, AMRO was for commercial enterprises. In addition, there were specific savings banks, specific mortgage banks and so forth. This is no longer the case.

If you compare the Dutch banking industry with the sector in Italy or Spain, for example, it immediately strikes that these countries count a far greater number of financial institutions, while margins are also much higher. So the fact that there are many providers in Spain and Italy does not lead to sharper competition and tighter margins; on the contrary. This leads me to conclude that clustering as such does not by definition lead to reduced competition.

On top of this, increasing regulations also demand transparency. There are regulations concerning the financial statements, concerning supervision, particularly the supervision exercised by institutes such as NMa and DNB. In a word, careful watch is kept that no cartels are formed.

Thirdly, the "all-finance" concept is an attractive strategy because connections can be made. At the same time, it is a vulnerable strategy. Someone always can come up with a niche strategy for a particular market. There are, for instance, small companies, even with as few as one, two and three staff, which concentrate on financial planning and investment advice. They are our competitors, more than other banks. And I also expect growing competition from Internet entrepreneurs who provide simple products.

To put it briefly, the "all-finance" strategy, which uses the advantages of a combined products and offers customers a so-called total solution, is under continuous pressure. Competition will only become more intense.'

We assume that these large entities are easy to control, but some 'accidents' have happened recently.

Mr. Van den Goorbergh: 'Regulations compel transparency contributing to fewer risks, which may disrupt the system. If financial institutions have to publish more information about their market risks, this in itself leads to a reduction of the risk profile. Certainly if it is supported by well-organised supervision.

And that is indeed a possible problem area. There is a constant race between financial innovations and adequate supervision. It can be argued that of the 100 financial innovations, 98 are in fact arbitration on existing regulations; whether the regulations of supervisors – solvency supervision or liquidity supervision, for example – or the regulations of the tax authorities.

Despite the fact that accidents occur now and again, the system of international supervision and international regulations has in any case preserved us from really severe shocks on the financial system until now. Some time ago there was a brief threat that things would go wrong with LTCM, but what happened was that the international monetary authorities indeed did their duty.

The issue of the "moral hazard" is becoming more insistent. Large financial institutions can actually afford to take more risks because they know that they won't easily be allowed to go bust. Their loss would bring about a domino effect that no one would permit to happen. The only correct response continues to be international information and consultation, good contacts between supervisors, firm measures against managers of financial institutions seeking the limits.'

Shouldn't national governments and institutions like the European Central Bank and the Bank of International Settlements play a greater part in the supervision on financial institutions than they do at present?

Mr. Van den Goorbergh: 'I think so. However, I also think that the focus point of control over financial institutions should remain with the national authorities. But they have to ensure an international system of agreements is in place, that will produce a level playing field. And the exchange of information will have to be optimised so that any problem with a financial institution is quickly communicated to other countries.

A form of bank supervision which is delegated to one or another body in Basel, Frankfurt or even the United States won't in my view produce much advantages. Between supervisor and supervised a certain relationship must grow so that they can properly understand one another. If the supervision becomes too far detached and becomes anonymous and bureaucratic, those supervised tend to act in a rather legal fashion and with less involvement. For supervisors it then becomes much more difficult to take "discretionary decisions".'

So your relationship with the Dutch central bank involves mutual consultation. What is your opinion on the supervision of financial institutions in other EC countries. The Maastricht Treaty explicitly defines this as a national task?

Mr. Van den Goorbergh: 'We have some experience with this in other countries and it is very dissimilar. In my view supervision must be tailor-made. I am an advocate of the subsidiarity principle. The lower you can organise something, the better it is. In other words, you must have a strong argument for centralising supervision in the financial industry, because you always loose knowledge of one another in the process of centralisation. Of course, you also gain with it: an increase in scale does have advantages; a larger playing field offers more possibilities. Therefore, I am not against centralisation, but subsidiarity must be the point of departure.'

With powerful players like the existing ones, can the ECB pursue a real monetary policy?

Mr. Van den Goorbergh: 'In the context of European unification it is very important monetary policy is pursued at the European level only and that it is removed from the span of control of national governments. These should only be concerned with budgetary policy and with wages policy. Monetary policy should thus be excluded from the political arena.

A national monetary policy and an exchange rate policy actually no longer exist. As a result, the full force of competition comes to rest on wages. I still consider wages policy to be an instrument of government policy, although it often comes about in negotiations between employers' and employees' organisations. Governments attach increasing importance to the regulation of the level of wages because their possibilities for adjusting exchange and interest rates are no longer available. Other instruments thus are more heavily laden if you want to achieve the same objectives. As a matter of fact, this was already asserted by Tinbergen.'

How do the major strategic decisions come about at the Rabobank Group?

Mr. Van den Goorbergh: 'In principle, strategic decisions are a task of the executive board. Our starting point for those decisions is the need of our customers. For example, at one time we saw that customers who came to us for savings and loans also considered life and non-life insurance products to be important. When we concluded that we also had to supply insurance policies. That's when we incorporated our insurance company Interpolis.

Later on we saw that our customers increasingly wanted to invest in investment funds, shares, bonds. We then entered into a strategic alliance with the Robeco Group and subsequently acquired it.

When our customers wanted to participate in international funds transfers, wanted foreign exchange products, asked for trade financing, we made sure we had it in place as well. Our lending grew much faster than our savings permitted. We filled in that gap via the international money and capital market. We must be active on those markets to fill the need of our customers for our lending.

In the near future we see decollectivisation and privatisation in the field of social security. Pensions and other retirement provisions therefore come into play, various schemes for personnel with a different form of financing. Because we envisage a growing need in these areas we are developing a policy in this field.

Our previous chairman Mr. Wijffels once said: "The creation of strategy at the Rabobank is actually extremely simple: you only need to examine the development in the requirements of customers; the only complication is that you must look five to ten years into the future". To put it briefly, that's what I mean by customer focus. We reason on the basis of our customers' market.

Incidentally, I have to admit that when you acquire companies you also acquire their customers. By taking over the Robeco Group we also gained its customers. So we do not have a stable customer base. As a result, the analysis of the development of customer needs must be adjusted at regular intervals.

We take the customer focus rather than the point of view of shareholders' value. It should, however, be pointed out that the two approaches are not too dissimilar and "at the end of the day" even come quite close. But that is because of the competition. Competitive relationships in the market eventually bring companies together in the same marketplace and prices converge there.'

Which instruments do you use for planning your strategy?

Mr. Van den Goorbergh: 'Our Strategy Department is continually performing competitive analysis studies. Furthermore, within the organisation we have departments that thoroughly analyse the various business sectors and transmit all kinds of signals from the outside.

You could say that on the one hand we have some of the characteristics of the Anglo-Saxon system with "outside" and "inside" directors, although the Anglo-Saxon system does not have a Supervisory Board above this like we do. In fact, our board consists of two bodies: the "Executive Board" and the "Board of Directors". The latter is made up of people who should represent the outside view. Over these two bodies is the "Supervisory Board". Other Dutch financial institutions usually have the classical NV (public limited liability) structure with an executive board and a supervisory board.'

The rules and practice of corporate governance state that it is important an organisation is transparent. Does Rabobank, as a non-listed company, find transparency important?

Mr. Van den Goorbergh: 'Certainly, and not only with respect to external corporate governance but also for internal corporate governance. The public and those within the organisation should know where and how business units are placed.

We are very transparent in every respect. One of the most important characteristics of our co-operative nature is that we maintain a constant dialogue with our members, in fact our customers. Therefore, there are few possibilities for hiding things. By its very nature this structure exacts considerable transparency.'

How does the bank measure 'customer value'?

Mr. Van den Goorbergh: 'One possibility is to ask customers whether they appreciate our products. Furthermore, we examine whether the market accepts what we have on offer. Thus market shares are very important to us. We may consider "customer value" to be of paramount importance, but if eventually only 1% of the Dutch population does business with us, that is not very significant. Market shares, changes in them, benchmarking – how do our products compare to those of other providers – that is what we want as indicators.

In addition, we naturally use classical financial indicators to determine whether something is up to scratch. But as I already said, at the end of the day, it is competition that brings together this approach.

Incidentally, I think that a competitive system improves when there are parties present with a different focus. If every player in the market pursues shareholder value, the tendency towards consolidation, even cartelisation is much greater than when there are parties present which do not only focus on shareholder value. In countries where strong co-operative companies operate, prices are generally lower than in countries where there is no major co-operative player. They form a kind of "counterveiling power", sometimes this is referred to as the presence value of the co-operative. It is not very easy to prove, but it is easy to understand that it works in this way from a theoretical point of view.'

Short-term interest rates in the Netherlands actually ought to be the same as those in Germany, but graphs produced in the past few months show that they increase differentially. Is this because of the transparency of the market, because the market in Germany is much larger than that in the Netherlands?

Mr. Van den Goorbergh: 'I am aware of the phenomenon: the differential is even greater than it was in the past. When guilders and D-marks still existed, the spread between them was lower than it is now. Incidentally, the differential had a tendency to vary somewhat, depending upon the thoughts of the financial markets about the chances of devaluation. Such a difference in interest rates cannot exist on the basis of economic rationality, but it does. It has everything to do with perception. Investors apparently think the German market is a more liquid market than the Dutch, despite the fact that this is not confirmed in practice. But if many institutional investors think so, then that is how it is.

If I were an investor for a pension fund, I would never include German debtors in my portfolio; I would only take Dutch ones because I would realise a higher return. There must be a time when the differential fades away. It is irrational that it continues to exist, but it may exist for a long time because of different perceptions. The fact that there is a difference between the interest on a bond issued by the Dutch state and one issued by a company is quite clear: a company can fail, so there is a debtor risk. But it is actually totally inconceivable that there is a debtor risk with respect to the Dutch and the German state. Nevertheless, that is what people think. You don't see this on the short side of the market – three-months and the like is all the same – but there is a difference in the longer term.

Where Italy is concerned, it is quite natural that the difference in rates is much higher. The thinking is as follows: I can buy 10-year government bonds, but I will still ask for a higher return because Italy may withdraw from the euro at some stage. It is interesting that this occurs, but it is in any case not something that we had expected.'

IT makes the market more transparent. Will the IT evolution have a major influence on the banking that we are used to? Where will the development of IT banks end?

Mr. Van den Goorbergh: 'You can call it "creative destruction". IT is turning the world upside down. Our bank has been fairly active with

Internet during the past few years. We introduce improvements every six months. It is now already possible to pay via Internet, place investment transactions and review your investment portfolio. This is a very interactive process and the expectation is that it will continue to develop.

IT in general is becoming crucial in banking, certainly in the area of the fairly simple products. Distribution by means of IT-applications is becoming more and more mainstream. It is customer demand which is the driving force behind this development.

Furthermore, from a viewpoint of cost effectiveness centralisation of IT-services is demanded. From a viewpoint of customer care all knowledge about a person should be available on his demand and the IT-systems should make it possible.

Both tendencies lay a heavy strain on IT-investments, but it is inevitable for a customer oriented approach.'

What will the Rabobank, and particularly the package it offers, look like in five year's time?

Mr. Van den Goorbergh: 'In five years, the "all finance package" will stand even more firmly on the domestic market than it does at present. In the field of "employee and company benefits" and to a certain extent also traditional insurance, we will certainly be substantially larger. This was also the thinking behind the merger we sought with Achmea.

Furthermore, we will have worked out a "multi-domestic" concept with a number of parties in neighbouring countries. Thus enabling internationally operating corporates and small and medium sized companies to make use of the services of Rabobank or her partners abroad.

A third element is that activities which by their very nature have a European or global scale – I am thinking of asset management and operating on the global financial markets – will be performed by clustered companies that are specially designed for this purpose. On the Dutch market we have an excellent starting position in this respect. Nevertheless, a lot of work will have to be done.'

Epilogue

The purpose of the epilogue is to reflect on the interviews that were held on the subject of Strategic Finance. When choosing the persons to be interviewed, an attempt was made to find a balance between the theory and practice of strategic finance. A balanced mix was found between people with ultimate financial responsibility in the real world and scientists who study the theoretical backgrounds. In this way a comprehensive picture is provided of the state-of-the-art in the field.

Finally, it is also a good idea to look to the future in this epilogue. What is currently on the agenda for the Strategic Finance issues requiring attention in the short term? Such considerations are of course visionary, but it is all about extrapolating a number of historical trends. In any case, the subject of Corporate Governance is dealt with in more detail. The Peters Committee on Corporate Governance has performed important work and it is now essential to provide some follow-up to the forty recommendations. The business community has adopted the majority of these recommendations, but the crucial points about more and direct influence of the shareholder have not yet been sufficiently realised in the Netherlands. This problem must be solved. It is abundantly clear that the Anglo-Saxon influences will continue to increase throughout Europe.

Another point that will continue to demand attention is supervision. Through the Bank of International Settlements (BIS) progress is gradually being made to limit the financial risks in the international community as much as possible. The regulations resulting from this are exerting an influence. It also appears from this that no European country can behave as an island and that the statutory framework on which they base their operations has both a European and an international dimension. There are now a number of bodies charged with supervision from various perspectives. A redistribution of the tasks and responsibilities of the various supervisory bodies could have to take place in order to increase transparency. An important aspect on which the supervisors will have to focus is the prudent use of derivatives. The expectation is that their use will continue to increase in the future and the option approach will have repercussions on adjacent and new fields.

This brings us to the consequences of developments in society concerned with subjects from the field of Strategic Finance. The medium to give shape to this development is the function and design of the annual report. With a slight time lag, these developments have repercussions on external reporting. In essence there should not be any lasting difference between societal demands and the content of the annual report therefore. In the interviews reference is made to a number of trends in this respect.

A number of unsolved problems remain in the field of strategic finance, including the determination of the optimum capital structure among other things. At the moment, it is not so difficult for companies to find funding, but if the tide turns this subject will once again automatically receive more attention.

Considerable attention is paid to the subject of external developments in this collection of interviews and a number of internal developments are also referred to. Examples in this connection are the new insights into management reports, the 'balance scorecard' and 'value based management'.

It is also important here to touch on the influence of the 'new economy'. Information technology facilitates all kinds of changes. Are the laws of economics applicable in the new service economy or not? Is economic growth possible without inflation? Does the new economy lead to the 'law of constant or increasing returns'? In any event and whatever explanations are given, it is clear that information technology is one of the driving forces for changes in strategic finance.

Various interviewees deal with the subject of the euro. Economically speaking, the introduction of a single currency for the EMU area is of major importance. In the not too distant future, private individuals will be confronted with a new currency and monetary unit. This represents a significant psychological factor. The euro is currently depreciating against the dollar and the two currencies have now almost reached parity. This certainly does not mean it will remain this way in the future. Quite clearly the euro as a currency is internationally too weak against the dollar with the result that the political position of Europe is being undermined with respect to the US. One of the most important issues for the coming years is how the euro will develop. Therefore, no further economic integration can take place without further simultaneous political integration.

An important aspect is that there is increasingly a link between corporate strategy and Strategic Finance. One of the reasons for this is the pursuit of shareholder value, which is regarded by many companies as a guiding principle for the business activities and the 'real option' approach, which makes it possible to apply techniques like options in

180

fields other than the financial decision-making process. It therefore appears that the financial function will be increasingly important in the management of organisations.

Finally, a few words should be said about the more fundamental aspects. In this context, responsible – financial – management should ultimately be guided by good and fair administrative practices administration. Although all kinds of subjective opinions can be given to explain this term, it is all about ethics. The opinions in question are subject to change and fashion over time. Although by no means exhaustive, the aspects include: providing full disclosure, the prevention of market deterioration caused by insider trading, effectively and efficiently managing scarce financial resources, taking account of the prudence principle, keeping segregation of duties and maintaining the quality of information.

Luc Keuleneer
Dirk Swagerman
Willem Verhoog

Editors' biographical information

Willem Verhoog (1950)

Willem Verhoog has been the Secretary of Royal NIVRA's Continuing Professional Education Committee (VERA) since 1 August 1974. In

1971, he became a fully qualified teacher at 'De Driestar' in Gouda. In 1974, after having worked for a few years as a teacher in Alblasserdam/Kinderdijk, he joined Royal NIVRA where, upon the occasion of his 25th anniversary in June 1999, he was presented a liber amicorum with 25 professorial contributions.

Mr. Verhoog is responsible for the development and progress of continuing professional education provided by the VERA. In this capacity he also participates in a pan-European CPE study group that produces European-wide workshops.

Due to his ability to build bridges and develop networks, the VERA succeeded within the twenty-six years of its existence in putting together and delivering a fully-fledged CPE package with more than 100 seminars and a few thousand participants each year. Mr. Verhoog is editor-in-chief of the monthly 'VERA Actueel' journal, editorial board member of 30 different NIVRA publications, joint editor of the VERA study series 'Actualiteiten in accountancy' and co-author of a series of books produced by the VERA in each of which fifteen experts in a particular field of finance discuss their own particular field of specialisation. This book, *A Vision for the Future, In Conversation with Financial Strategists*, is the eighth publication in the series.

Dirk Swagerman (1949)

Dirk Swagerman studied at junior technical school and was subsequently admitted to a school for higher general secondary education. In 1969, he started as a non-degree student at the former Municipal University of Amsterdam and also followed evening classes leading to a successful completion of state examinations and initial degree programme in 1971. In 1975, he was awarded a degree in public administration. He subsequently gained a master's degree of Business Administration at Michigan State University and, following a management consultancy postgraduate course, the title of Master of Change Management. At Stanford University he participated in the Senior Executive Program in 1989 and the  Financial Management Program in 1999. In 1991/92, he qualified as Master of Business Telecommunications at the University of Delft.

Mr. Swagerman has been a management consultant for most of his working life, with activities mostly being related to the organisation and design of the financial function. Recently he obtained the degree of PhD at the University of Twente with a thesis about the application of IT in the financial function. He is a member of the Dutch Association of Certified Management Consultants, the Royal Institute of Engineers and the Association of Public Administration. In addition, he is associated with Deloitte & Touche in Amsterdam and part-time associated with the department of Financial Management and Business Economics and the department of Management of Information Systems of Twente University.

Luc Keuleneer (1959)

Luc Keuleneer has a Commercial Engineering degree from the Catholic University of Leuven (1981) and a Master's degree in Business Administration (Finance) from the University of Chicago (1983).

He started his career as a research assistant in the Finance department of the Catholic University of Leuven and was later attached to the same university as fellow of the National Fund for Scientific Research.

Following this, Mr. Keuleneer worked as an advisor in the cabinet of the Minister of Economic Affairs and Finance, as management attaché at Paribas Bank and as director at the Insituut der Bedrijfsrevisoren. He was also vice-chairman of the Executive Board of the CGER-ASLK Holding company and director at CGER-ASLK Bank. He was also a member of the privatisation committees of both the Belgian Federal government and the Flemish government. He was also managing director at Deloitte & Touche Corporate Finance.

At the moment, Mr. Keuleneer is director at KPMG Corporate Finance Brussels. He is also director and member of the audit committee at GIMVINDUS, Werfinvest, Finindus and Sidinvest.

Furthermore, he is adjudicator in the Brussels' Commercial Court, Professor in Financial Management at the Free University of Amsterdam and the University of Gent, lecturer at the Catholic University of Leuven, senior lecturer at the University of Maastricht, University of the Netherlands Antilles, VLEKHO Handelshogeschool in Antwerp and at the Royal NIVRA.

In addition to these posts, he is a member of the editorial board of the 'Tijdschrift Financieel Management' and the 'VBA Journal'.

6861   97